Enterprise Rules

Important and timely ... A must read for anyone concerned with effective, high achievement organisation and management with positive implications for the future of work and society.
Gareth Morgan, Distinguished Research Professor, Schulich School of Business, York University, Toronto

Don Young's book should be required reading in all our business schools and boardrooms. If capitalism in the Anglo Saxon world is not to become consumed by its own excesses, straight dealing, thrift and ethics need to make a comeback quickly, and Young aims to shove the business world firmly in that welcome direction.
Lord Monks, former General Secretary of the European Trade Union Confederation and of the UK Trades Union Congress

Don Young's very readable, and often profound and amusing book is to be welcomed for emphasising the ethical and human aspects of business as critical ingredients in fostering high achievement, and for placing learning at the centre of business strategy.
Alastair Wilson, Chief Executive, School for Social Entrepreneurs

Most of the books offering recipes for business success should be left on the shelf. Don Young's very accessible new book is the exception and should be read both by managers and anyone interested in the purpose of business and management.
Karel Williams, Professor of Accounting and Political Economy, University of Manchester

Packed with wisdom and experience and good ideas ... The best book I have read on management for a long time.
Mike Haffenden, Co-founder and Director of the Corporate Research Forum (CRF) and the Performance and Reward Centre (PARC)

Full of common sense and practical guidance ... will help us all rise to the challenge.
Robert Napier CBE, Chairman of the Homes and Communities Agency and former Chairman of the Met Office

First class on the essentials required for sustainable business growth ... its valuable insights and practical frameworks will help take business thinking away from the current narrow preoccupation with the short term.
Mike Regan, former Group HR Director of Electrolux and NG Bailey

A penetrating analysis of what drives value in business ... and a must read book for executives, investors and all those who set the corporate framework.
Paul Hewitt, Chairman of OB10 and a Director of Kiln Insurance and The Co-operative Banking Group

An excellent catalyst for the shift required to get enterprises focused on delivering long-term sustainable financial returns and fair treatment of all stakeholders.
Robin Keyte, Director, KEYTE Chartered Financial Planners

Read this book. It could act as a spur to finding ways of making people's lives more satisfying at a time when there is so much unrelenting gloom.
June Barnes, Chief Executive, East Thames Group

Extremely interesting and often amusing, I haven't read a better book on the integration of the economic, social and political aspects of management ... To be recommended to managers and students of management alike. That many of the traits of the high-achieving companies identified by Don Young reflect key characteristics of Scandinavian culture is a 'happy coincidence' indeed.
Margareta Hult Gardmo, former head of the Department of Organisation and Management, Linnaeus University School of Business and Economics, Sweden

A rare, welcome and skilful combination of help on business self-analysis and the challenges in driving and achieving change.
Paul Chambers, CFO, Meridian Energy, New Zealand

Enterprise Rules

The foundations of high achievement – and how to build on them

Don Young

P

PROFILE BOOKS

First published in Great Britain in 2013 by
Profile Books Ltd
3a Exmouth House
Pine Street
Exmouth Market
London EC1R 0JH
www.profilebooks.com

A CIP catalogue record for this book is available from the British Library.

ISBN: 978 1 78125 116 4
eISBN: 978 1 84765 962 0

Typeset by MacGuru Ltd in Stone Serif
info@macguru.org.uk

Printed and bound in Great Britain by Bell & Bain Ltd, Glasgow

MIX
Paper from
responsible sources
FSC® C007785
FSC
www.fsc.org

Contents

Prologue

This is very much a book for today. It is hard to think of a time when people have felt so disenchanted with commercial enterprises, especially banks and newspapers; so distrustful of politicians and their advisers, so put upon by those that they consider are ripping them off and so unhopeful about their own futures. Religion with its promise of reward in the life to come is far less likely to provide consolation than in the past. Economic gloom, unemployment and anxiety about old age add to the general feeling of dissatisfaction and concern.

All the same, the vast majority of people still want to work and to do something worthwhile with their lives. Many studies have shown that most people are looking for meaning in work. Good employers who consciously seek to provide that meaning get high employee commitment. Many talented young people seek out work that can provide them with the satisfaction of doing something worthwhile. So canny employers and senior managers are starting to realise that they must take these pressures seriously: otherwise, in the longer term they will have less capable, less responsive workforces, unable to respond to the shifts and dramas of survival. They also know that they will not be successful with their customers in the medium term unless they can provide a convincing experience of good products, helpful service and responsible public behaviour.

Not all organisations are like the worst of the banking and media worlds. Excellent customer and employee focused ventures can be found in many places, even in banking, and public trust is high in less commercially focused ones, such as community interest companies and charities. Some organisations that are owned by their employees or customers, such as the John Lewis Partnership and the Co-operative Group, also engender confidence, as do many family companies. And what these organisations do is in no way mysterious or impossibly clever. Nevertheless, mythologies have been created by those who benefit by encouraging the rest of society to forget old wisdoms and instead put themselves in the hands of gurus, 'heroic' leaders, peddlers of expensive technologies and, worst of all, market manipulators.

The messages of this book are simple but hugely important. Organisations that manage to provide meaning for employees, satisfaction for customers and a net contribution to society can expect to prosper in the longer term. This has been known for a long time, ever since the nineteenth century and the Quaker entrepreneurs; but in the era of instant gratification, of celebrity without effort and of ridiculous wealth without responsibility, we have seen good things disparaged as 'boring' and have lost sight of what matters. Let's get down to the enduring foundations of high achievement and build enterprises that add value to people's lives and to the wider community.

Foundations

Values and assumptions – and a poke at a few sacred cows

Introduction

Let me start with a personal note. I was a manager for over 30 years and a consultant for six in companies I helped to found. My introduction to management was through the central graduate trainee scheme of Unilever, a global consumer products company. In those days some called the likes of me and my fellow trainees 'Crown Princes'. But Unilever was a wise company: its graduate trainees were sent to do real work at the front line. After eight years or so selling soap to grocers, working in fish and chemical plants in the UK and helping to run a trawler fleet in Newfoundland, I was wiser about notions of royalty. Working in factories was probably the most important experience of my life. And my most influential mentor ever was a supervisor called Stan Allison, who was the embodiment of practical wisdom. I now find it hard to conceive how anybody can be an effective top manager without the experience and insights generated by working at different organisational levels – from the 'shop floor' up. My own experience was enlivened in its middle and later stages by a growing predilection for working in large enterprises facing big problems. Most of these were a result of past mistakes and poor management by executives, often people with public reputations that belied their private deficiencies. The really proficient managers that I had the privilege of working with generally had lower public profiles and were little known in the wider worlds of the financial markets and media. Many were not British.

During a long career which saw me reach the top teams of three large companies, and co-found two smaller ones, I had the good luck to work with some of the best business gurus, many of whom are still active. In particular, I remember professors Jay Lorsch of Harvard, Henry Mintzberg and Gareth Morgan of McGill, Warner Burke of Columbia, Marcus Alexander of London Business School and Roger Harrison, a wise American consultant. The reason I remember them is that they had the courage to abandon their classrooms and come to work with groups of senior managers who were tackling difficult problems in real time. Most said they had not had such an experience before. Mintzberg wrote about it.

I have tried to express the wisdom of these worthies and Stan, as well as the experiences of working with some inspiring colleagues in companies that ranged from well-run industry leaders to basket cases. High on the list of learning experiences have been mistakes that I have made. The weakness behind many of these was a tendency to assume people could be coached to competence. Alas, I got it wrong too many times and learned the hard way to take good advice about appointments.

Sadly, in my later days I was witness to the growing influence of the investment markets over big quoted companies, and the consequent changes in the behaviour of managers at the top, which damaged long-term performance and sustainability.

Being instrumental in making an enterprise high achieving is immensely rewarding and worthwhile. As well as the financial benefits available to all stakeholders, economic success increases resilience, and enables investment for the longer term that will cushion against the inevitable shocks that will beset any organisation. But the story goes much further: sustainably high-achieving enterprises are more often than not rewarding for people to work in. They can enrich people's lives in ways that go far beyond financial success. There is good evidence to show that they are vibrant communities, creating purpose and meaning for many people, some of which extends into their personal lives. Thus they can also enrich a wider community – the creation of trusting relationships within such organisations is likely to spill out into a wider theatre. There is good evidence to show that sustainably high achievers generally add value to the communities around them and thus to the wider economy and society.

Unfortunately, there are too few of them left, especially in the UK. The ravages of 'financialisation', short-termism and 'creative destruction' – and political meddling in the public sector – have destroyed many a valuable enterprise and damaged others. Today, the best places of work are often to be found among smaller enterprises and organisations that are not subjected to the full blaze of investor and media scrutiny.

This book

Most management writing examines specific facets of knowledge and practice: finance, strategy, organisational behaviour, marketing and the like. Many business school programmes are similarly organised. I once attracted unfavourable attention at INSEAD, a business school, by commenting that the structure of its programmes seemed to match the organisations of the large bureaucracies that provided most of the students.

This book is different because it is based on the fact that good managers have been shown not to think in specialist 'silos'. It examines the roots of high achievement from many angles, and then pulls the various strands together into integrated action programmes.

The second part looks at the relationships between organisations' external and internal environments, and the way they are run from the board through to middle management all the way to the 'front line', with a view to integrating the whole enterprise.

In seeking to provide an understanding of high achievement it looks at the following perspectives:

- Economic: discussing value creation, financial and socio-economic aspects.

- Psychological and social: examining the vital and often underused contributions of the social sciences.

- Political: considering organisational politics and the uses and abuses of power.

The third part, the Workbook, contains self-use material that should provoke readers to consider the strengths and weaknesses of their own enterprises, and, if they wish, plan and implement their own programmes of change and performance improvement.

Finally, the appendices include three profiles of enterprises that by and large live by the messages or 'rules' of this book – and are prosperous and happy places to work. Evidence that shows that the ingredients needed to create high-achieving enterprises are a portion of flair and an enormous amount of effort and attention to detail. The journey has no end but many twists and turns. High-achieving enterprises usually have a sense of destiny; they never relax in their efforts; they know that the road ahead is full of opportunities, surprises and not a few challenges. The most successful forms of growth are those based on incremental innovation and improvement coming from rich veins of experi-ence rather than sudden spurts of inspiration or ego-driven big deals. In many ways, the journeys of accomplished top managers and their organisations are similar to those described by John Bunyan in *The Pilgrim's Progress*. The road to success and salvation is long and often winding, and there will be tempta-tions aplenty to leave the high ground; but those who remember what really matters and are true to themselves and others are the ones whose enterprises will eventually win the prize of sustained high achievement.

High achievement is a product of the dedicated efforts of everybody, not just a special few. High-achieving enterprises attract the commitment of all their staff and the support of customers and other stakeholders in equal measure.

The top managers most likely to support sustained achievement bond with their organisations, listen to the wisdom of other people, especially those on the front line, and have sensitive antennae to detect strong and weak signals denoting changes, problems and opportunities. There is much evidence to say that the best managers regard strategy as something they work at all the time. They believe in experimentation, in many small initiatives, and not grand plans. They also use all their senses and are respectful of 'hard' data, but they would not dream of acting on it without going and checking by personal observation what is really happening.

But there are many ways of ruining good enterprises. Neglect of the organisation, egocentricity, autocratic and bullying behaviour, getting cut off from the real world, rushing into deal-making as a first resort and complacency are just some of them. Inept or uncaring top managers can, with a little help from a small number of 'advisers', ruin enterprises very quickly.

The book is based on a number of fundamental premises:

■ There are no standard 'recipes' that apply to all enterprises. Each one is unique in terms of its history, culture and context.

■ A working knowledge of a range of social and economic dimensions is essential to success. Overemphasis on any one is likely to cause damage.

■ It is essential to understand the roots of high achievement and have a good understanding of organisations, people, markets, finance and power in organisations.

The characteristics of high achievers

I have chosen to focus on 'high achievement' rather than 'performance' because achievement has the connotations of something that is built up to through training, hard work and dedication. Like successful sports teams and athletes, high-achieving enterprises are not created overnight and they need to keep working, learning and adapting to sustain their success.

What differentiates high achievers from others is examined in Part 2, but here are some of their characteristics:

■ They achieve alignment between and satisfy the needs of all their stakeholders – staff, customers, owners/investors.

■ They do this in a timeless way; their economic performance enables them to invest for the long term.

■ They are resilient and can ride difficulties, as well as profit from good times.

■ They are attuned to their environments, constantly adapt and learn from experience.

■ They are internally aligned, with close bonding between staff at all levels. Information passes easily up, down and across the organisation.

■ They create positive meaning for their staff, through pride, relationships and generating a sense of doing good.

■ But getting hands-on in your own organisation is what really matters. It's like the difference between understanding food science and practical cooking.

1. Sense and nonsense

The phenomenon of management as a topic worthy of serious study is relatively recent. The beginning of the twentieth century saw the emergence of serious research into the nature of organisations and their leaders. Henri Fayol and Frederick Taylor both applied scientific methods to studying the nature of leadership and the organisation of work. Much earlier, Adam Smith postulated that the division of labour would make large-scale production possible and efficient – and Max Weber developed the concept of bureaucracy as a means of organising in government and industry.

The evolution of the business school brought with it the notion of management as a serious professional activity. The modern business school developed in the United States and spread rapidly through the Anglo-Saxon world of business – rather less so in Asia and continental Europe.

For a time, scientific management became popular. Rigorous and methodical long-term planning using stringent analytical constructs was all the rage for a time. Managers were exhorted to respect the primacy of hard data and be on top of the numbers. Robert McNamara, as US defence secretary during the Vietnam

War, wanted only 'hard' data and revealed the dangers of getting cut off from direct experience, from intuition or 'feel', and thus from reality.

The post-war period has seen an explosion of research and thinking about enterprise and leadership. There has been a thread of rigorous investigation that has sharpened understanding of the realities of management. For example, research by Rosemary Stewart, Jay Lorsch, Gareth Morgan, John Kotter and Henry Mintzberg among others has exploded the myth that organisations are neat hierarchies obeying tight rules – and that good managers behave in an orderly manner, applying scientific methods to forecasting, planning, organising and so on. Acute observers like Peter Drucker and Charles Handy, who based their writing on research evidence, confirmed these findings.

But alongside such insightful and stringent research has come a huge explosion of what might be described as quasi-religious material, often pushed by 'gurus'. This has given rise to a number of dubious ideas, among which several stand out:

- The development of such concepts as visions, missions and values. In some respects, much of this is harmless, but it has given rise to the creation of rigid 'templates' requiring followers to spell out the vision, the mission, the values, the guiding principles and the strategies. While this approach may help to clarify some issues, taking it too seriously can get in the way of crafting real strategies.

- The religious theme has been accentuated by the popular notion of the charismatic leader, who can transcend reality by sheer willpower and personal magnetism. This concept of leadership gained traction in the 1970s and was personified by Lee Iacocca, the legendary (in his own mind at least) chairman of Chrysler in the 1980s, and more recently by Jack Welch, late of General Electric.

- Associated with charismatic leadership have been the positive psychology and New Age movements, which combine theological notions with mysticism. In essence, followers believe that the power of thought can affect the material world beyond the self. This thread of ideas has spawned all manner of movements and gurus who can enable followers to become rich, successful and powerful simply by willing it.

This chapter seeks to sort some of the nonsense from common sense in providing a durable understanding of factors that contribute to high achievement.

Some enduring wisdom

In praise of realism

Much management bookshelf material is based on an underlying premise – not always made explicit – that once the rationale, methodology or 'recipes' that will guide readers to the path to high performance are understood, the way forward is clear. It's a bit like having a satellite navigation system in your office – a clear voice will guide you on your way.

Why challenge this premise? Because it seems to me that much of the 'help' available is not clear enough about the complexity, length or arduousness of the journey towards high achievement. Because much successful change and progress is not the result of carefully planned and executed strategies – it is the product of small steps, experiments, trying many things together and learning from both successes and failures.

The art of high achievement in business has parallels with high-achieving sports teams or athletes – those who do well have talent, but in reality, they practise and train more than the also-rans. Sustaining high achievement is not easy; it requires the commitment of the whole organisation, not just a special few. A lot of the bookshelf material is misleading, some of it is sheer rubbish – and most of its recipes are not easily transferable from one organisation to another. So learn from your own and others' experience and then create your own bespoke programmes.

Some difficulties on the road to high achievement are as follows:

- Changing requirements will almost inevitably create casualties – those individuals who cannot make the grade, or whose values become at odds with those required for progress. These casualties will occur at every level in an organisation, including the very top: often managers who may have been appropriate in the past become blockages to progress in the future. Failure to face up to such difficult issues and manage them skilfully and with consideration will hobble efforts to change.

- The real world is messy and often unpredictable. Progress may become stalled, pressures and opportunities may change. At such times, adaptability is crucial and finely judged decisions will need to be made in order to continue as planned, slow down or change direction.

- Any long-term programme of change and improvement is a journey into unknown territory. There needs to be continuous review and feedback to keep everybody in tune with progress, priorities and emerging discoveries. Otherwise confusion and dissipation of effort may result.

- The road to high achievement will be strewn with obstacles as a result of personal rivalries or disagreements over strategy among managers. Different elements in the organisation may choose to misunderstand each other, tribal 'fiefdoms' may stand in the way of progress, and individuals may play subtle power games that have nothing to do with furthering the enterprise's objects. Leaders require considerable political skills and sometimes may need to be brutal in dealing with – even getting rid of – opponents.

Who learns wins[1]

A guiding philosophy of this book is that learning and action skilfully melded together are a powerful mechanism for promoting sustainable high achievement. So, how might this idea work in practice?

The late Reg Revans, a professor at Manchester Business School, developed a groundbreaking thesis that most traditional management training, based on teaching and didactic methods, was by itself an ineffective way of helping managers to learn. He argued that good managers had a predilection towards doing, and that sitting in classrooms studying cases and listening to presentations by learned people were insufficient for guiding the actual practice of management. So he devised a method of learning based on a cycle of action and reflection that led to learning and insight – and thus to more insightful action. This cycle, he argued, was more appropriate to the environment that most managers lived in and to the nature of the managerial animal.

Revans argued that learning had two key components: programmed learning, taken from established bodies of knowledge, and action learning, derived from active experience and questioning. I am not denigrating programmed learning; it provides the essential basis of any professional activity. But without active application and questioning it is insufficient in a complex and changing world. Indeed, there is a sound body of evidence to demonstrate the performance-enhancing virtues of using learning to inform action and action to feed learning.

Learning can also occur on an organisation-wide scale. It is unlikely that organisations will be sustainably successful unless they are open to learning both from their own experience and that of others. Revans produced a learning formula:

$$L> = C$$

Where
L = the rate of learning
C = the rate of change in the environment

Some assumptions behind the action learning philosophy

- People learn best by facing the challenge of having to do something real
- Formal instruction – delivered far from the point of action in content and temporally – is inadequate in providing the wherewithal to act appropriately in real time
- Urgent problems or enticing opportunities provide a good spur for learning
- Practical learning can best occur through trying things (action), receiving feedback and reflection, leading to more insightful action
- Reflection is best facilitated by seeking the inputs of others with different perspectives
- Involving many people both in tackling problems or taking opportunities and in reflection leading to widespread learning and more insightful action is the key to organisational learning
- Organisation-wide learning and action are the key to sustainable success. Experimentation and learning are the best bases for strategic thinking and action

This holds that the rate of learning in an organisation must be equal to or greater than the rate of change in its surrounding environment. If the learning rate inside is less than the rate of external change, the organisation will decline or die.

In a complex and ever-changing environment, learning is at the heart of effective strategy formulation and implementation. The 'root and branch' approach to strategy, which advocates determining an overall objective and then by analysis formulating a pyramid of increasingly detailed goals, objectives, targets and action programmes to achieve it, has proven to be fatally flawed. But this has not stopped governments, aided by consultants, trying to manage such activities as the improvement of health, policing and education services. The results have been disappointing.

In 1959, Charles Lindblom described the art of 'muddling through'. He contrasted the root and branch approach with a more oblique method of 'building out from the current situation, step by step and to small degrees'. (And involving many people in the process to elicit their experience and ensure alignment.)

Muddling through is a rather downbeat way of describing a powerful process of action, reflection, learning and adaptation that seems best tuned to the contemporary environment for public and private enterprise alike. Effective strategy formulation and execution are at root learning processes.

Values – an invisible guidance system

Everyone has a system of values and organisations need a clear, shared and sound set of values and guiding principles if they are to become high achievers. Some of the values embedded in the arguments of this book as necessary for an organisation to be a high achiever are as follows:

■   **Enterprises are human communities and must embody mutual respect.** People are the only creative and innovative force. Losing sight of this can be hugely destructive. Most of the wisdom and skill in organisations is embedded in the wider workforce. It is wrong to underestimate the contributions of the many through a bias towards an elite. Leaders who ask questions to learn will do better than those who issue orders. Successful enterprises foster many leaders at all levels and do not rely on a few heroic figures.

■   **There is such a thing as 'society'.** Humans are social animals. We have become dominant on the planet because of a special ability to work collaboratively and form communities and organisations to achieve complex tasks. Trust between individuals and groups has been shown to be the vital glue that makes the achievement of complex tasks possible without coercion and excessive monitoring – thus reducing costs.

■ **All enterprises should contribute towards the wellbeing of society.** In general, the point here is that businesses should serve a wider community than, say, just shareholders and employees. If organisations cause harm to the world around them, they are to be condemned, no matter how effective they may be. In this way, the Mafia, undoubtedly a highly successful organisation, can be discounted as a good example for others to follow. Equally, enterprises that damage the fabric of society or the planet are to be denigrated.

■ **Learning is the key to sustainable success.** Most people are naturally curious and exploratory and keen to learn. But many organisations squash the creative spark. Leaders have a responsibility to encourage creativity in others and to support learning. They can best do this by engaging extensively with staff and being open to learning themselves.

■ **It is better to act, learn and adapt than seek perfection.** In a complex and constantly changing world, it will never be possible to assemble perfect information to guide decisions and action. It is better by far to act on the best information available. The consequences will provide an opportunity to learn and adapt future actions. This value lies behind Lorsch's 1970s observation: 'Successful strategic change tends to be incremental and often exploratory. It is mostly based on experience and subjective judgement, rather than rational analysis.'

■ **Collaboration is more important than competition.** This may conflict with prevailing contemporary values about the benefits of competition and needs further elaboration. The values behind this statement are as follows:

  – Complex tasks require the collaborative efforts of many people with different skills. Conflict and competition inside enterprises can rapidly derail them.
  – Competition should be limited to activities that can benefit from variety and choice, without creating too much waste and duplication. These activities are much more limited than free marketeers would claim – for example, large organisations delivering health services need a high degree of internal collaboration to ensure learning and the maintenance of consistent standards.
  – Selfish individualism when practised to benefit one person at the expense of others is damaging and despicable, especially if hidden behind a cloak of altruism.

■ **There is more to motivation than money.** The obsession in certain quarters with pay and bonuses is an aberration. Most people will work with commitment if they believe that the money is fair and the purpose worthwhile, and if they trust their leaders. A growing body of research shows that, above a basic standard, happiness is rarely obtained by increasing wealth.

A value system for high achievement: the Quaker influence

Some of the highest achievers in the nineteenth-century world of business were the great Quaker entrepreneurs. Their influence on railway development, iron and steel manufacturing, banking and – of course – confectionery was fronted by such men as John Cadbury, Henry Rowntree, Sampson Lloyd, Abraham Darby and many others. William Lever, founder of Unilever, although not a Quaker, adhered to many of their beliefs. In America, William

Penn and many nonconformist entrepreneurs also founded great businesses on similar values. Their values were contrary to prevailing behaviour. Workers were often treated as cannon fodder, subjected to terrible treatment and paid starvation wages. So, when the great Quaker entrepreneurs became rich and powerful as a result of their 'out of line' behaviour, it became known as 'the happy coincidence'. Behaving ethically and treating people with dignity actually begat wealth.

The beliefs and practices of these great entrepreneurs are not some quaint historical relic. They are as vibrant and alive today as they were in the nineteenth century. This is borne out by contemporary research on the foundations of high achievement, which indicates that the fundamentals of lasting success have not materially changed. But, as in the nineteenth century, there are many who have forgotten, or ignore, the roots of lasting achievement in the restless search for quick fixes, novelty or instant enrichment.

What was distinctive about the Quakers?

The following are extracts from a talk given by Sir Adrian Cadbury in the 'Faith Seeking Understanding' series in May 2003.[2]

- **They inspired trust.** This was linked to their refusal to swear on oath, based on the biblical injunction against swearing. But fundamentally they believed that there could not be two standards of truth. Truth was truth. This led to their success as bankers, because banking depends on trust. It also meant that the price they put on their goods was the one at which they intended to sell them. This was in contrast to the prevailing custom of haggling over prices. It was an ethical approach but also good business – and caused resentment among their competitors. Most people prefer to know they are not being fleeced, rather than to have to bargain to achieve the same end.

■ **They saw life as a whole – religion was not just for Sundays.** One of the 'Queries' Quakers are asked to consider is: 'Do you maintain strict integrity in your business transactions and in your relations with individuals and organizations? Are you personally scrupulous and responsible in the use of money entrusted to you, and are you careful not to defraud the public revenue?' They must be unusual among Christian groups in giving specific advice on business ethics. As a result, they supported each other and kept an eye on fellow Quaker business people, to maintain their reputation. When my great-great-grandfather came to Birmingham in 1794, to open his draper's shop in Bull Street, he went to Bull Street Meeting and met Sampson Lloyd to whom he had an introduction. The firm has banked with Lloyds ever since.

■ **Their unwillingness to support war opened up business opportunities.** The Darbys did not as ironmasters make cannon during the Napoleonic wars like their competitors. Instead, they developed a range of domestic ironware which turned out to be a far bigger and more stable business than armaments.

■ **Their respect for the worth of every individual influenced the way in which their businesses were managed.** I saw many instances of this at Bournville. It encouraged the view that everyone's contribution to the business was of value. This made for good working relations. Suggestions for improvements were welcomed and followed up, whatever their source. Because of their belief in equal worth, women played an important role in Quaker affairs from the outset. The same was true in our company where, in Edward Cadbury's day, women's departments were managed by women to ensure that they had a fair share of managerial posts. I have no doubt that the firm gained greatly from the belief that everyone working there had something of value to offer the enterprise.

■ **They believed it was important to make decisions by agreement.** Voting could mean that the views of minorities were disregarded and overridden. The aim was to arrive at a 'sense of the meeting'. In industrial relations, which was my field in the firm, it often meant considerable time spent in debate and argument, but it also meant that decisions once arrived at could be implemented quickly and with commitment.

■ **They were encouraged to look for a better way forward, rather than accept the world as it is.** This stemmed from the belief that you should follow the divine light within yourself. It made Quakers ready to challenge accepted practices and to innovate. The spirit of innovation was unintentionally assisted by one of the laws passed to keep Quakers and other dissenters in their place. The Five Mile Act of 1665 meant that Quakers needed to live more than five miles from established towns and cities, if they were to worship and to go about their trades freely. Birmingham was such a place and so became a centre for Quakers and nonconformists. There they had the advantage that they were not bound by the restrictions imposed by the guilds over matters like apprenticeships and methods of working. They were free to invent new products and new methods of production. A good example is Robert Ransome, whose firm makes lawnmowers to this day. In 1803, he invented the self-sharpening plough, which kept its edge as it wore. Then in 1808, to meet the problem that farmers tended to break their ploughs at the same time at the beginning of the season, he produced ploughs made of interchangeable parts. They could be quickly repaired by inserting new parts, instead of his having to repair the whole plough on site. In effect, he invented the process of mass production used by Henry Ford to make his cars.

▓ **They respected education.** They were excluded from much of the formal educational system. It was not until 1871 that Quakers and Catholics could enter Oxford or Cambridge. They started their own schools and needed to be literate if they were to carry out their mission. As a Quaker history rather stuffily puts it, their belief in education and study 'was an advantageous factor in the quality of mind of an important portion of their labour'. Thus they benefited to the extent that they employed fellow Quakers. Again, their approach to learning was not bound by ancient custom. William Penn, on leaving for America in 1682, set out his views on how his children should be educated:

> For their learning be liberal … but let it be useful knowledge, such as is consistent with Truth and godliness … I recommend the useful parts of mathematics, as building houses or ships, measuring, surveying, dialling, navigation, but agriculture is especially in my eye: let my children be husbandmen and housewives, it is industrious, healthy, honest and of good example, like Abraham and the holy ancients, who pleased God and obtained a good report.

History is not bunk: the lessons of the past are crucial

There is solid evidence that the foundations of high achievement have not shifted in three centuries. The principles on which the great Quaker and nonconformist entrepreneurs of the nineteenth century based their businesses are remarkably similar to those that contemporary research reveals as relevant today. The studies of André de Waal and others reviewed in Chapter 2 indicate that the foundations of high achievement are the relationships between people and customers and the values that underpin these.

Of course, there have been significant developments in understanding and business 'technology' since the nineteenth century, but most of these are peripheral to the foundation factors – and many new developments, such as the dominance of finance, are arguably harmful to long-term performance and sustainability. In fact, the cause of failure and disappearance of many originally Quaker enterprises has been the influence of the financial markets.

The world tends to move in cycles, one new thing supplanting another until the same fancies come round again, the same beliefs take possession of the minds of the herd and the same old mistakes are repeated. For example, the crisis that followed from the 2007 credit crunch occurred because those whose minds were turned by the moment somehow believed that they were living in a new age in which all the old rules and the nature of markets had changed forever. 'The end of boom and bust' even became the proud boast in 1997 of a British chancellor who went on to become prime minister.

In his famous book *The End of History*, which was published in 1992, Francis Fukuyama prophesied that the world had reached a perfected state in which democratic capitalism had triumphed – and 'Anglo-Saxon' free markets would rule the world. Events have proven him to be wrong.

The remarkable book *Extraordinary Popular Delusions and the Madness of Crowds*, written by Charles Mackay and published in 1841, should be compulsory reading in every bank and boardroom and every economics and MBA course. Mackay describes a succession of crazes and episodes of mass madness that led to such phenomena as the South Sea Bubble in 1720. It is hard to argue that the dotcom bubble and the current financial crisis are any different.

We have a lot to learn from history and historical trends as they help us to understand human behaviour and the relationships between economic, environmental, social and political factors. Learning from history requires the ability to synthesise and form patterns from different kinds of data. People weak in this ability – and therefore unable to learn from history – will never be good strategists and are unlikely to make good leaders in a complex world.

Studies reveal the uncomfortable fact that most strategic errors are not new; they are simply repeats in one form or another of previous cycles. Many have not learned that large acquisitions have at least a 60 per cent chance of destroying value or worse. Or that leaders who owe their allegiance primarily to psychologically distant investors in the financial markets are likely to end up causing great damage, as we have seen from the age of 'shareholder value'.

Management is famous for its attraction to fads, with new ideas being adopted with gusto and then dropped when it is discovered they aren't all they are cracked up to be and have harmful side effects – by which time there is another new idea that has become the rage.

The new is always exciting. That is understandable. But a bit more reflection on the past before dashing to join the herd of neophytes is likely to lead to a more successful future.

Obliquity and the virtues of the indirect pursuit of goals

Rentokil and its CEO, Clive Thompson, were once the darlings of the UK stock market. The company's stratospheric growth in profits, around 20 per cent year on year, caused Thompson to be dubbed 'Mr Twenty Percent' by admiring investors and media. The seemingly miraculous performance was reported by insiders to have become an obsession. The company pushed relentlessly to maintain its rate of profit growth. But after the crash, it became apparent that staff had been underpaid and driven beyond their limits of endurance, customers had been exploited and investment neglected.

Now, think of reversing the process. If Rentokil had supported and developed its staff, innovated to provide excellent customer service and invested in product, systems and staff support, it is probable that it could have been highly profitable over the long run. Ten years after the crash, the company is still slowly recovering from the disastrous 'Twenty Percent' period.

The point of this story is that long-run success is not achieved by obsessing about profit or any single goal, but by oblique means – meticulous attention to the factors that will contribute to long-run success and thus profit. Of course, it is possible to maximise profit in the short run by squeezing all costs and savagely cutting investment. In days gone by Hanson Trust did it, but its business model, maximising shareholder returns by squeezing acquisitions dry, eventually ran out of steam and the group was broken up. Single-minded pursuit of shareholder value eventually ruined the company and all who pursued that goal.

As John Kay points out in his book *Obliquity*, the same applies to happiness.[3] It appears that the happiest people are those who pursue goals and activities that fulfil them, not happiness *per se*. In my experience, flying a light aircraft well in difficult conditions makes me feel happy in retrospect, but I am not conscious of seeking happiness when struggling to land in a strong cross wind. Hence for most people the combination of sufficient money, achieving important goals, having deep and satisfying relationships, and being successful in a chosen field of work will in combination result in a sense of satisfaction and therefore happiness. Those who pursue happiness through doing what others want them to – for example, shopping 'til they drop – do not report lasting happiness.

Charles Handy describes another dimension of obliquity. In a 2002 *Harvard Business Review* article, 'What's a business for?', he writes:

> Both sides of the Atlantic would agree that there is, first, a clear and important need to meet the expectations of a company's theoretical owners: the shareholders. It would, however, be more accurate to call most of them investors, perhaps even gamblers. They have none of the pride or responsibility of ownership and are, if the truth be told, only there for the money. Nevertheless, if management fails to meet their financial hopes, the share price will fall, exposing the company to unwanted

predators and making it more difficult to raise new finance. But to turn shareholders' needs into a purpose is to be guilty of a logical confusion, to mistake a necessary condition for a sufficient one. We need to eat to live; food is a necessary condition of life. But if we lived mainly to eat, making food a sufficient or sole purpose of life, we would become gross. The purpose of business, in other words, is not to make a profit full stop. It is to make a profit so that the business can do something more or better. That 'something' becomes the real justification for the business. Owners know this. Investors needn't care.

The truth of Handy's words is borne out by the poor performances of the many companies that espoused the pursuit of shareholder value as their primary goal.

Success will come not from pursuing the goal of high achievement for its own sake, but by being clear about the assorted activities that together will lead to sustainable high achievement. This means having a strong sense of deeper purpose and taking care of money, customers, staff, innovation and many other variables. The chairman of Unilever got it right when he said in 2011 that the company's main job was to satisfy customers and develop staff, not to please shareholders.

Some illusions

Super leaders

An earnest executive search consultant once told me that there was a small number of people of such talent that they could transform the fortunes of any organisation lucky enough to obtain their services. Needless to say, they were worth huge sums of money. He went on to mention a number of household names. Is this true or mainly fantasy?

There have always been superstar leaders who dominate their organisations. In the past they were often the people who had started the business and built it up, whereas today they are usually hired hands. Examples in recent times include Jack Welch of GE, John Browne of BP, Clive Thompson of Rentokil and Lee Iacocca of Chrysler. There is little doubt that all these people were talented, but to read the eulogies, it is possible to believe that they possessed supernatural powers, slew dragons and were single-handedly responsible for their business's successes.

As Rakesh Khurana, a professor at Harvard Business School, has commented, the new kind of CEO is expected to provide a vision of a radically different future and to attract and motivate followers for a journey to a new promised land. Such heroes are supposed to have the gift of tongues and be able to inspire employees, investors, analysts and the press. But, says Khurana, charisma, like its close relative, romantic love, can be blinding, with severe consequences. The first trap is what psychologists describe as the 'fundamental attribution error'. There is little evidence, except in exceptional circumstances such as a severe crisis, that a CEO's impact has a fundamentally positive effect on the performance of a large organisation. Studies indicate that up to 60–65 per cent of a business's performance is attributable to industry and economic effects, and much of the rest to the strengths or weaknesses of the wider organisation and deep competencies within it. How can a single person, usually with a short tenure, have a lasting positive effect on these fundamentals? But they can have a negative impact – destruction can be wrought more quickly – through one big deal, for example.

And one effect of the 'fundamental attribution error' is to lessen the tenure of a CEO because, if the great hero fails to save the day, he or she is likely to be replaced.

Another mistake is that of attaching great significance to extraordinarily superficial descriptions of people. Khurana describes the deliberations of a board appointments committee, which attached tremendous importance to a candidate's strengths because he 'had worked for Jack Welch'. Similarly, many Americans believe that Ronald Reagan 'won' the cold war and that Alan Greenspan 'ran' the American economy. On the other side of the Atlantic, many people seem to believe that prime ministers 'run the country'.

Most evidence tends to show that leaders in sustainably high achieving companies come in all kinds of shapes and sizes; tend to bond with their organisations and lead by example and involvement. Most would deny heroic status and hand the credit to the whole organisation.

Khurana summed up the hero genre in a *Harvard Business Review* article, 'The Curse of the Superstar CEO', in September 2002: 'Yet today's extraordinary trust in the power of the charismatic CEO resembles less a mature faith than it does a belief in magic.' Wise words!

Super organisations

Three examples – Enron, GE and Marconi – amply illustrate the illusion of super organisations with transformative abilities. In their book *Power Failure: The Inside Story of The Collapse of Enron*,[4] Mimi Swartz and Sherron Watkins (who was a vice-president at Enron and is considered by many to be the whistleblower who helped uncover the scandal), say:

> [The people at Enron] were purveyors not of products but of ideas, of what Jeff Skilling called 'intellectual capital'. A company didn't need bricks and mortar to triumph in the new age. It needed smarts – smarts that, as Skilling liked to claim, would propel Enron from its old role as the World's Leading Energy Company to its destiny as the World's Leading Company. So far, Enron's numbers were on track to do just that: to land Enron in the top ten of the Fortune 500. Third-quarter revenues had grown over 150 per cent from the prior year's corresponding quarter to $30 billion, bringing total revenues for the first nine months of 2000 to $60 billion – up $20 billion from 1999. The company's stock had quadrupled in value since January 1998 to almost $90 a share. In just five years, Enron grew to rival 1990s tech giants like Cisco and Microsoft, and behemoths like GE. It was a media darling: Fortune magazine hailed Enron as the country's most innovative company for five years in a row, and included Enron in the top quarter of its list of the 'Best 100 Companies to Work for in America'.

Enron was, in short, a company of winners. At the dawn of the twenty-first century, those who were bright, young, and fiscally ambitious were reassessing their career choices. They could slave away in some fusty commercial bank or corporation for years at a salary in the high five figures. Or they could join a Wall Street investment bank, where they could make a lot of money but never really create anything of value. Silicon Valley was great, but it was overrun. And then there was Enron. Those who packed their bags and raced to Houston were the ones who wanted to run their own show right away – by the time they were twenty-five, their salaries were commensurate with their genius.

Through the leadership of the legendary Jack Welch and the introduction of a range of leadership practices – Six Sigma, Organisation Work-out, ABC registers and Session C Reviews (C-rated managers were invited to seek careers elsewhere), organisational 're-invention' (through an in-company unit called 'Destroy your Business') – GE was 'transformed' from a ruthless cost-cutter to a leading-edge, world-class learning organisation. On top of all this, internal boundaries were dismantled so that learning and new ideas could be seamlessly transferred across the whole organisation.

But what did GE really do? A research project on GE conducted by a team from the Centre for Research on Socio-Cultural Change (CRESC) and the University of Manchester between 2004 and 2006 concluded the following:[5]

Our analysis of the undisclosed business model is relatively straightforward and focuses on 7 Principles of GE's cost recovery under Welch:

1. Run the industrial business for (maximum) earnings
2. Add industrial services businesses to cover the hollowing out of the industrial base
3. Buy and sell companies to achieve returns and growth objectives

4. Rely on large-scale acquisitions to prevent like-for-like comparisons and to increase (financial) opacity and the power of (the management and organisation) narrative
5. Grow the financial services up to the limit of the company's credit rating
6. Accept the balance sheet costs in terms of (low) returns on capital
7. Add financial engineering to smooth earnings and manage growth

This is quite a different story.

Furthermore, in 2009 the *Wall Street Journal* reported that Jack Welch accepted 'that the obsession with short-term profits and share price gains that has dominated the corporate world for over 20 years was "a dumb idea". Welch offered this remark before news that GE, which he left in 2001, had been downgraded by Standard & Poor's, losing the pristine Triple A rating it had held since 1956.'

On the other side of the Atlantic, Marconi emerged from the chrysalis of the old General Electric Company (GEC), a rather grim conglomerate that had been dominated by Lord Weinstock for many years. Weinstock was, to put it mildly, financially conservative and built a huge cash mountain. On his demise, George Simpson, who had been CEO of Lucas Industries, took over. Simpson appointed John Mayo, a hugely ambitious finance director with a banking background, and the company embarked on a remarkable 'transformation'.

In essence, they sold most of GEC's defence businesses – and with this, plus the cash pile Weinstock had accumulated, embarked on a massive acquisition splurge with the declared aim of placing Marconi at the forefront of the emergent and convergent mobile communications market.

Marconi's 2000 *Annual Report* gives a vivid flavour of the kind of 'visionary' strategies that can be created by a small group of people at the top of an organisation:

Marconi is pursuing a once-in-a-lifetime opportunity to transform communications and knowledge management. The moment is unique because right now, the landscape of communications and information is being transformed beyond recognition.

The Marconi Vision.

Marconi intends to drive the transformation and convergence of communications and information.

We will add relevant information and knowledge management to our customers' businesses. We will meet the needs of carriers by defining the new public network.

In this way, we will profit and grow, supplying the picks, shovels and maps of the new internet gold rush.

By 2001, Mayo, then deputy chief executive, and Simpson, egged on by mainly enthusiastic investors and the media, were celebrating a good transformation job well done. He said in the annual report of that year:

Since 1997, we have made the transition from slow-growth conglomerate to fast-growth technology company.

Fully Integrated Company.

Going forward, we will manage Marconi as a fully integrated company, not as a conglomerate … Our new divisional organisation is up and running, management is in place and we are already selling solutions.

Shortly after, the company collapsed amid accusations that it had attempted to conceal the scale of the financial disaster caused by its strategy. Simpson and Mayo were ejected and the company was broken up, leaving behind a massive destruction of value. In short, an ill-conceived and ill-executed transformation strategy had destroyed a company that had taken generations to build. Real transformations of established companies are rarer than hens' teeth.

Lessons

▪ If an enterprise's performance seems too good to be true – it probably is.

▪ Most innovation in larger organisations is incremental, not revolutionary. Revolutions normally come from individuals and tiny organisations.

▪ Every organisation is unique – and in many ways. Each will have different histories, cultures, competencies, strengths and weaknesses and structures. Furthermore, it will operate in different environments and contexts. Therefore the idea of 'patching' across leaders, best practice or case learning from one to another is fraught with difficulty. And difficulties become huge risks if the intent is to use another organisation's transformation as a template.

▪ Cases and examples are fine as a general basis for discussion and thinking, but should not be slavishly copied, unless the best practice applies to something very simple and procedural.

Management is not a science

Why is it that much research insight generated down the years seems to be ignored by so much of the establishment in business, government, education and the professions?

▪ Why is numerical data regarded in many quarters as more accurate than hands-on understanding based on direct observation and feel?

▪ Why do some organisations – UK government departments especially in recent decades – become so fixated on target-setting and numerical measurement of performance?

▪ Why are so many powerful people seemingly hell-bent on pursuing strategies that seem to be destructive of organisations as social and moral entities that can elicit the creativity and commitment of all their members?

Some of the reasons were convincingly demonstrated by the late Sumantra Ghoshal, a professor at INSEAD and London Business School. The essence of his argument is that there has been an increasing focus on applying the principles and methods of the physical sciences to the practice of management, and that this has no doubt been influenced by the enormous income that a large number of business academics and consultants have been able to generate from peddling the idea that reality can be reduced to metrics.

This has resulted in:

■ an overemphasis on finding principles, rules and models that will have universal application;

■ a faith in quantification and numerical measurement as being the only reliable manifestations of reality and the 'truth';

■ a deep assumption that everything that matters can be understood through scientific principles (Ghoshal describes this as 'the pretence of knowledge');

■ widespread assumptions that there are natural laws that will determine outcomes;

■ beliefs that people will respond only to inducements and punishments and that in terms of motivation they are primarily concerned with material self-interest.

The implications of viewing management as a science are profound:

■ Anything that is not susceptible to finite quantification is rejected. Thus enterprises are not purposeful communities propelled by human intent. They become bundles of assets that can be bought and sold.

- Leadership by forming relationships and inspiring people by contact, dialogue and coaching is thoroughly suspect. It is better to measure compliance with governance rules.

- Top managers should not bond with their enterprises and form lasting emotional commitments. They should pursue shareholder value creation and retain a degree of independence from their organisations.

- The assessment of people becomes 'psychometrics', measuring fragmented facets of individuals and then trying to build a picture of the whole person. Dialogue-based and biographical approaches to assessment are viewed in many quarters as suspect because they rely too much on human judgement and not enough on quantified measurement.

- The moral and ethical bases of work are undermined by the ethos of what matters is what works, whatever the methods used to get there.

- Learning becomes the transmission of formal bodies of knowledge to the uninitiated through teaching. Success is marks in an exam, which is of course formally validated by a superior authority. Learning by action, reflection and experience is not capable of being formally examined and therefore of suspect value.

- Ordinary employees are treated as powerless pawns and no longer encouraged to make their unique contributions or to take emotional ownership of their work.

In short, human inspiration, ideas, emotional commitment and creativity are not taken into account because they cannot be measured, placed into an index, modelled or represented on a spreadsheet.

Creative destruction – a dangerous concept

The world is full of theories, some based on careful observation and proven by research, others without any serious foundation.

One theory that has received much attention is that 'creative destruction'[6] is a necessary condition for a healthy economy.

It is presumably based on a fusion of neoliberal free-market economic theory and the theory of evolution, but not on any substantial evidence in its application to enterprises. Some species do indeed die out, to be replaced by stronger ones. But what is not taken into account is that the species that survive and thrive have always adapted to changes in their environment – in other words, they have learned to cope with or take advantage of changing circumstances.

To apply 'nature in the raw' ideas to human enterprises is dangerous, because humans, individually and in communities, can learn and adapt – and, more importantly, anticipate changes in their environment.

It seems to me that the concept of creative destruction originates from a particularly bleak form of economic determinism, which allows no room for the human spirit. Destruction is not inevitable, and the destruction of human communities that have the potential to learn and adapt is neither beneficial nor desirable.

Of course, some enterprises will die or go into decline and atrophy, but in the majority of cases this is not a predetermined inevitability, unless an organisation's fundamental purpose becomes obsolete. Atrophy and death usually occur because of neglect, mismanagement, ignorance, collusions to ignore crucial information, complacency or destructive behaviour – and none of these are 'creative'.

The antidotes to atrophy, decay and destruction are not difficult to find; they are learning based on an active curiosity about the world and a resolve to adapt and change as threats or opportunities arise in the external environment. In an ever-changing world, individuals and communities must adapt; those that do not are likely to stagnate and die. In the world of enterprises decay can be almost imperceptible in its early stages. This often happens in organisations that have been successful for a long time and fail to notice new competitors, changing technologies, customer expectations or fashions. Such declines are usually gradual but over time deterioration accelerates and the end, if it comes, can be sudden.

IBM became complacent and stuck in the 1980s, as did Marks & Spencer. Both nearly failed and had to be radically turned round. The turnarounds took ten years or more. Examples of companies that signally failed to adapt are Woolworths, Polaroid, Pan American, TWA, Bethlehem Steel and Kodak, and in the UK Plessey and Thorn Electrical Industries.

Thus it is important to have an appreciation of the dynamics of destruction and renewal and not assume that destruction is creative.

Things to beware of

Most people have special hates. Here are some of mine:

■ Gurus and writers who purport to be able to change your life if only you tune in to their 'secret discovery'. Deepak Chopra and Rhonda Byrne are good examples of the genre. The following quote about a Byrne book gives a good flavour:

> For the first time, all the pieces of The Secret come together in an incredible revelation that will be life-transforming for all who experience it. In this, you'll learn how to use The Secret in every aspect of your life – money, health, relationships, happiness, and in every interaction you have in the world.

Chopra is a leader in the genre that promises success by following what at first sight might be seen as platitudes. Francis Wheen says in his book *How Mumbo Jumbo Conquered the World*:[7]

> It [Chopra's advice] suits New Agers seeking the 'inner self' – and high achieving materialists who like to think that fame and riches are no more than their due, reflecting the nobility of their souls. Chopra is happy to oblige them: 'People who have achieved an enormous amount of success are inherently

very spiritual.' Vain tycoons and holistic hippies alike can take comfort from Chopra's flattery ('you are inherently perfect'), and from his belief that the highest human condition is 'the state of "I am": Since we reap what we sow, both health and wealth are largely self-generated.' Following this logic ad absurdum, he argues that 'people grow old and die because they have seen other people grow old and die. Ageing is simply learned behaviour'. For celebrities – and many others – Chopra offers a metaphysical justification for smug self-absorption, and requires no effort or sacrifice.

William Ian Miller, author of *Losing It*,[8] was clear about his views on such stuff: 'These fields are either culpably moronic or a swindle.' Among what I consider to be dangerous techniques are EST (Erhard Seminar Training), which seeks to rebuild people's psyches into more positive forms, creating dependency on the cult. Some of these cultish beliefs have invaded the world of enterprises and in my view should be vigilantly guarded against.

■ Psychological inventories that are not supported by face-to-face counselling. There are some excellent inventories, such as the Myers Briggs Preferences Inventory, but even this produces results that may be mysterious to recipients without good coaching.

■ The mathematical modelling of enterprises, which are actually human communities and not susceptible to such approaches. No wonder most economists completely missed the impending financial crash, a result of human greed and incompetence. Random stock selection would produce the same results as many institutional investors.

■ Misuse of statistics, as practised by politicians, lobbying bodies, companies and advertisers (for example, '9 out of 10 women prefer XXX').

■ Business journalists who regurgitate corporate spin and especially tales of the deeds of business superheroes without investigating the truth of them. Also a tendency of business media and literature to reduce complex enterprises to one person.

- Jargon is the last refuge of the shallow thinker or self-important manager; those who talk about 'paradigm shifts', 'tremendous synergies', 'silo thinking' or 'holistic solutions' while they are 'pushing the envelope' or 'thinking out of the box' or trying to 'square the circle' are usually generating more vapid hot air than sense.

- 'New paradigms' – an almost sure sign of a guru on the make. Enron marked a high point of new paradigmism, being characterised as a new breed of 'White-Haired Revolutionary'. The dotcom boom was often described as reflecting a new paradigm – until it went bust.

- 'Five minute' solutions and '5 steps to …'. Alas, the worlds of organisations and the human behaviour in them are not susceptible to such mindless simplicities.

- Consultancies that use their stars to sell and their gophers to deliver at 'star' rates. External help can sometimes be useful, but the most important thing is that organisations learn from external intervention and are able to cope on their own next time. A light leavening of external help followed by self-managed improvement projects is generally the best way to use consultants. I once worked for an organisation that commissioned 26 McKinsey studies at a cost of millions and did nothing about any of them.

- Consultancies that purport to be able to perform tasks that belong to organisations and people who use them. For example, governments and companies have used large consultancies to 'implement' strategies. Consultancies are not built to implement; managers are (or should be).

- HR departments that create onerous human-resources systems out of a misplaced belief in a theoretical 'good practice'; and flabby line managers who let them do it

because they haven't the balls to deal with real people
issues.

■ Search consultants who are more influenced by the
look and speech patterns of a candidate than a serious
assessment or evidence of their previous performance; and
a tendency to assume that candidates who have worked for
a much-admired company must be good themselves.

2. Perspectives

As the management industry has burgeoned, so has interest in discovering what makes for 'good' enterprises. The trouble is that the search for 'secrets', 'new paradigms' and heroic deeds has created a huge amount of noise but few useful insights. This chapter attempts to identify significant indicators and characteristics.

Management thinkers

André de Waal

André de Waal, a professor at Maastricht School of Management, conducted a major search of all the evidence and research literature between 1990 and 2007 on what distinguished high-achieving commercial organisations. He considered about 280 studies and concluded that about 10 per cent of them were rigorous enough for their findings to be seriously considered. Some of the rest were used to add flavour. He came to the conclusion that:

> [High achievers] achieve financial results that are better than their

peer group over a longer period of time, by being able to adapt well to changes and react to these quickly, by managing for the long term, by setting up an integrated and aligned management structure, by continuously improving their core capabilities and by genuinely treating their employees as their main asset.

De Waal identified a number of common high performance factors:

- Management quality, which encompassed inclusive behaviour, lack of social distance and engagement with the wider organisation.

- Openness and action orientation, which included internal dialogue, openness to adaptive change and experimentation.

- Long-term orientation, which included financial conservatism, investment for improvement, growing their own managers and sustaining relationships with customers.

- A culture of continuous improvement, including progressive innovation of products and practices.

- Workforce quality, including appropriateness to task, dedication to results, high support and continuous learning.

From this research it is evident that high achievers are more than short-term money machines for enriching their leaders and institutional investors. They have broader purposes than simply making money, generating commitment from their staff through emotional attachment and providing meaning in their working lives.

Arie de Geus

Arie de Geus was director of strategic planning at Royal Dutch Shell, one of the world's largest companies. As well as its size, it has also enjoyed a long and successful life, being founded in the

1890s and growing from Anglo-Dutch roots. (This is one possible reason for its long life – the Dutch have not taken to notions of shareholder power like the British.)

De Geus led a fascinating study for Shell into the roots of sustainable success. He and the Shell team reviewed available information about companies that had survived longer than Shell, eventually studying 27 in detail.

In his book *The Living Company*,[1] he says: 'After all our detective work, we found four key factors in common':

- Long-lived companies were sensitive to their environments. As wars, depressions, technologies and political changes surged and ebbed around them, they always seemed to keep their feelers out, tuned to what was around them.

- Long-lived companies were cohesive, with a strong sense of identity. No matter how diversified they were, their employees (and even their suppliers at times) felt they were part of one entity. Case histories repeatedly showed that strong employee links were essential for survival amidst change. This cohesion around the idea of 'community' meant that managers were typically chosen for advancement from within; they succeeded through the generational flow of members.

- High-achieving enterprises managed to be efficient and innovative at the same time. They managed routine activities tightly, but also encouraged all employees to think of creative ways of bringing improvement and innovation.

- Long-lived companies were conservative in financing. They understood the value of money in an old-fashioned way; they knew the usefulness of having spare cash in the kitty. Having money in hand gave them flexibility of action. They could pursue options that competitors could not. They could grasp opportunities without first having to convince third-party financiers of their attractiveness.

It did not take De Geus and the team long to notice the factors that did not appear on the list. The ability to return investment to shareholders seemed to have nothing to do with longevity. The profitability of a company was a symptom of corporate health, not a predictor or determinant of corporate health.

Jay Lorsch

Jay Lorsch is one of the most eminent business academics of our times. In the early 1980s, he and Gordon Donaldson conducted a major research programme to try to identify what differentiated the best of American business leaders from the average and also-rans. One of the more interesting facets of the book was their description of the values held and enacted by these top managers. This is particularly fascinating because what Lorsch and Donaldson found in the 1970s seems to match almost exactly later research into the same subject from the early twenty-first century. This indicates that while the world at large has become more and more short term in orientation, this does not apply to high achievers. The tenure of top managers in high-achieving enterprises is lengthy, whereas it has decreased markedly in other large companies, especially those where external investor influence has been strongest.

One of the more powerful pieces in their book, *Decision Making at the Top*,[2] is their description of the values of highly successful corporate leaders, as compared with the commonly held assumptions, which they describe as popular 'myths'.

First, they state that there is a mythical assumption that the most successful top managers move between companies quite often. Not so, say the authors; the top managers of their industry leader sample had very long service, averaging well over 20 years. Then they describe a series of commonly held assumptions about the top managers of highly successful companies, comparing them with the reality that their investigations revealed (see table).

Myth	Reality
Successful top managers are driven to maximise shareholder wealth	Successful top managers are most concerned about the long-term success and survival of the corporation
Strategic decisions are crucially subject to capital market disciplines	The most successful companies seek to minimise their dependence on capital markets
The most successful top managers are mainly concerned with investor reactions and expectations	The top managers of the most successful companies are most concerned to be highly competitive in their product markets and to meet the needs and expectations of fellow employees
Successful top managers are mainly concerned about short-term results	Top managers in the most successful companies are most concerned with long-term corporate survival
Successful top managers are hungry to do corporate deals and make acquisitions	Successful top managers are most concerned to build their business organically but will make limited acquisitions to strengthen a market position
Strategic choices and decisions are rationally conceived and executed	Successful strategic change tends to be incremental and often exploratory. It is mostly based on experience and subjective judgement, rather than rational analysis

Sources: Donaldson, G. and Lorsch, J., *Decision Making at the Top*; author's notes at a Lorsch seminar

James Collins and Jerry Porras

In researching their book *Built to Last: Successful Habits of Visionary Companies*,[3] James Collins and Jerry Porras selected a group of sustainably high-performing 'visionary' companies and a group of 'comparison' companies not in the same performance league. They then systematically compared the differences between them and came up with a range of characteristics and behaviours that differentiated the 'visionary' set.

Included among the 'visionary' sample are such companies as Boeing, Ford, Johnson & Johnson, Marriott, Motorola, Procter & Gamble, Sony and Walmart. The main criterion for choosing these obviously successful companies was exceptional long-term performance.

Their 'visionary' (effective and durable) companies exhibit the following features:

- **Deeper purpose.** Top management and staff firmly believe that their enterprise has a reason for existence that goes deeper than 'just making money' or 'just satisfying shareholders'. The fundamental purpose of these companies is not to maximise shareholder value, but to make or supply something that is significantly useful to customers.

- **Strong core values.** One of the key characteristics of effective companies is that they are extremely flexible and responsive to change, apart from changes that would undermine the core 'ideology' of the company.

- **Stretching goals and innovation.** They are extremely ambitious when it comes to innovation, audacious projects and risk-taking, provided that these do not challenge the core ideology or risk the whole company.

- **Distinctive culture.** They have a commitment to a strong and enveloping culture, to the extent that the authors describe them as 'great places to work only for those people who buy into the core ideology; those who don't fit with the ideology are ejected like a virus'.

- **Active and experimental.** They are described as 'trying a lot of stuff and keeping what works'. The authors observe that they indulge in 'high levels of action and experimentation – often unplanned and undirected – that produce new and unexpected paths of progress and enable visionary companies to mimic the biological evolution of species'.

■ **Growing their own leaders.** A major and significant feature is 'home grown management'. According to Collins and Porras, the best companies promote from within, bringing to senior levels only those who've spent significant time steeped in the core ideology of the company. I attended a lecture given by Porras. He said that there was strong evidence that effective leaders did not need to be 'charismatic'.

■ **Culture of continuous improvement.** Last and obviously, given the above, the companies studied exhibited a 'relentless' pursuit of self-improvement, with the aim of doing better and better 'forever into the future'.

Investors

Investors who are serious take time and care to develop an in-depth understanding of the enterprises in which they invest. Once they understand the business, its products, processes, people and organisation, and have taken a view on its competitive strengths and weaknesses, they then invest for the long term, taking an active and involved interest in what the company is doing to maintain and improve long-term performance.

Warren Buffett and his partner, Charles Munger, are examples of superior investors, who have also included Benjamin Graham, John Maynard Keynes, Philip Fisher (all major influences on Buffett) and who have tended to follow broadly similar philosophies.

The 'golden rules' of these focus investors, as quoted by Robert Hagstrom in his book *The Essential Buffett*, are as follows:[4]

■ Concentrate your investments in outstanding companies run by strong management.

■ Limit yourself to the number of companies you can truly understand. Ten is a good number; more than twenty is asking for trouble.

■ Pick the very best of your good companies and put the bulk of your investment there.

■ Think long term: 5–10 years minimum.

■ Volatility happens, carry on.

Claude Bébéar, chairman and founder of AXA, a French insurance giant, has written a book entitled *Ils vont tuer le capitalisme* (*They Will Kill Capitalism*).[5] In it he proposes that it is time to remind the average investment manager that investors have duties as well as rights, and he argues that those who take a nurturing interest in companies and hold shares rather than churn their portfolios and bet on share prices should have special voting rights.

These behaviours can be vividly contrasted with that of the average 'active' fund manager. One such manager confessed in an interview with the author in 2003 to having 'on average less than half a day each' to evaluate information on the investments in his portfolio, let alone prospective ones. He went on to say that his prime focus was to take a gamble on what will happen to short-term share prices.

The views of focus investors like Warren Buffett on the habits and behaviour of the bulk of the investment community are encapsulated in a comment by Benjamin Graham, after attending an investment conference: 'I could not comprehend how the management of money by institutions had degenerated from sound investment to this rat race of trying to get the highest possible return in the shortest period.'

The family effect

Credit Suisse, an investment bank, is one of a number of organisations that have studied the performance and characteristics of family-influenced companies. 'Family-influenced' means that family owners have a sufficient stake to override or block the wishes of other shareholders should they feel they are not in the interests of the business. Well-known family companies include BMW, Cargill, Carrefour, Fiat, Ford, Hyundai, IKEA, LG Group, Michelin, J. Sainsury, Samsung, Toyota and Walmart.

The bank's studies indicate that companies with a consistent, long-term involvement of a family interest seem to perform on aggregate 8–10 per cent better on all major financial criteria than 'pure' quoted companies. Impressed by what it found, the bank set up a new investment fund, the Credit Suisse Families Index.

The Credit Suisse findings are typical of investigations in the field. The bank concluded that the main characteristics of the higher performance of family companies that differentiated them from mainstream companies are as follows:

- **Longer-term management focus.** Family shareholders usually require their managers to have a long-term strategic focus. Since most families intend to pass on their holdings to their descendants they have strong grounds to keep them in good condition, so their interests lean towards the longer term.

- **Better alignment of management and shareholder interests.** Families usually control a limited number of companies and those assets represent a material share of their wealth. As a result, families tend to focus intensely on the way a company is managed. In many cases they appoint a representative, often a family member, who sits on the company board with the aim of improving corporate governance and influencing the company's strategic orientation.

■ **Focus on core activities.** Companies with a significant family interest tend to keep their focus and activities tightly defined. This helps them avoid the pitfalls of overambitious, value-destroying acquisitions, extensive use of leverage and trendy short-lived strategies.

The Credit Suisse findings are supported by other studies. Akira Suehiro, a director of and professor at the Institute of Social Science, University of Tokyo, discovered that the best-performing Thai companies included family-owned enterprises and the worst performers were public companies that followed traditional free-market governance practices imposed by the World Bank.

■ 'The Dilbert Principle'

The material in Scott Adams's book *The Dilbert Principle*[6] is drawn from real experiences of American office workers who e-mail Adams their experiences of how they are managed. It provides a wonderfully humorous and ironic counterweight to the more serious management gurus who seek something much more portentous.

Here is some of the wisdom that Adams has gleaned from his correspondents:

■ Companies with effective employees and good products usually do well. Ta-daaa!!!

■ Any activity that is removed from your people or your product will ultimately fail or have little benefit.

■ Leaders spend their time concentrating on 'visions' of the future. This can take many forms, as long as nothing tangible is produced by the process. Through this activity the leader hopes to convince employees of the following:

   1. The leader knows the future and has agreed to share it with the company instead of using this awesome power to make a fortune gambling.

2. The chosen direction is somehow not as obvious as you think, so you are lucky to have the leader at any price.

Dilbert's ideal enterprise: the OA5 Company

OA5 stands for 'out at five'. Adams says that the primary objective of this company is to make employees as effective as possible:

> I figure that the best products come from the most effective employees, so employee effectiveness is the most fundamental of the fundamentals. The goal of my hypothetical company is to get the best work out of the employees and make sure that they leave work by five o'clock.

An OA5 company isn't willing to settle for less productivity from employees, just less time. The underlying assumptions for OA5 are:

- Happy employees are more productive and creative than unhappy ones.

- The average person is only mentally productive for a few hours a day no matter how many hours are 'worked'.

- People know how to compress their activities to fit a reduced time. Doing so increases their energy and their interest. The payoff is direct and personal – they go home early.

- A company can't do much to stimulate happiness and creativity, but it can do a lot to kill them. The trick is for the company to stay out of the way. When companies directly try to sponsor creativity it's like a bear dancing with an ant. Sooner or later the ant will realise it's a bad idea, although the bear may not.

A selection of OA5 practices

- Eliminate the assholes. Nothing can drain the life-force out of your employees as much as a few assholes who seem to exist for the sole purpose of making life hard for others. It's OK to be tough and it's OK to disagree – even shout. That's not being an asshole. Some conflict is healthy. But if you do it with disrespect, or you seem to be enjoying it, or you do it in every situation – you're an asshole. And you're gone.

- Make sure that your employees learn something every day. Ideally, they should learn things that directly help the job, but learning anything at all is to be encouraged.

- Support requests for training even when it's not directly job-related.

- Share your knowledge freely and ask others to do the same, preferably in small digestible chunks.

- Support experimentation sometimes even when you know it's doomed (if the cost is low).

- Imagine a job where after you have screwed up your boss says 'What have you learned for next time?' rather than 'What the hell were you thinking?'.

Many managers are obsessed with 'the big picture'. They look for the big picture in vision statements and mission statements and quality programmes. I think the big picture is hiding in the details. It's in the clothes, the office supplies, the casual comments – in what people do and how they spend their time.

Finally, Adams says:

> Creativity is allowing yourself to make mistakes. Art is knowing which ones to keep. Keep your people fresh, happy and efficient. Say what you want and then get out of the way. Let them come to you if they need help. Let art happen. Sometimes idiots can accomplish wonderful things.

Drawing the threads together

Combining the insights revealed so far with the experience of those interviewed for this book, there is broad consensus on the fundamental characteristics of high-achieving enterprises and the various dimensions that matter.

Key dimensions

- **Economic.** High-achieving enterprises are economically productive and/or use resources effectively. They show a balanced regard for the needs of customers, staff and owners/investors.

- **Temporal.** They do not have long- or short-term perspectives; they have a sense of temporal continuity, understanding that the short and the long term are both important. Their motto might be 'Do what needs to be done now but always anticipate and invest for the future'.

- **Customer-serving.** They regard the satisfaction and anticipation of the needs of their customers and clients as being of primary importance and as creating the means to meet other goals, such as rewarding owners and investors. They build solid relationships with customers and suppliers.

- **Givers of meaning to employees.** They need the long-term commitment of employees and achieve this through consideration and recognition of people. They emphasise the virtues of common purposes and fairness.

- **Contributors to 'society'.** Internal values of consideration and fairness spill over into their impact on the communities in which they are based. This does not necessarily mean that their products are ethically pure, but they do show a sense of responsibility for the effects of what they do to community and environment.

Fundamental characteristics

■ High-achieving enterprises show a dedication to their fundamental purpose, differentiating this from secondary outputs. Mostly, this purpose will relate to their core customer-serving mission, which also gives meaning to the work of all staff and generates commitment.

■ They are financially conservative (or prudent), investing for the long term – as well as, if not before, rewarding owners or investors.

■ They demonstrate strong values, which act as a binding force, creating a sense of common purpose and cohesion.

■ There is a strong bond between top managers and staff at all levels, forged by personal contact and dialogue, leading to a sense of fairness and trust. They are highly communicative, with few barriers and minimal withholding of information.

■ They 'know themselves' and are grounded in reality, but they have a sense of destiny.

■ They are highly attuned to their external environment, adaptive, curious and committed to learning.

■ They are willing to take risks and experiment, but do not 'bet the farm' on big deals or risks.

■ They grow their own talent. Top managers know the business and organisation well.

■ They never sacrifice the long term for short-term expediency.

None of this is 'new'

The research evidence shows that the fundamentals that lead to high achievement are timeless, subject to small steps of innovation, not to quantum leaps or new paradigms. It is apparent also that the huge changes in information technology and electronic communications have not changed the fundamentals. People have remained people. Organisational research shows no new forms over those revealed by Henry Mintzberg and Gareth Morgan decades ago. The obsession with shareholder value has failed to deliver lasting high performance, as shown by the unimpressive long-term aggregate performances of the UK FTSE 100 and US S&P 500.

Clearing and opening the mind

So, the first step towards high achievement is to clear away the rubbish, forget the search for instant solutions and free the mind to be receptive to creative ideas and effective strategies. This is the responsibility of those in or aspiring to leadership positions. They should question the contemporary norms and preoccupations and espouse a degree of humility, recognising the wisdom that resides in their staff and customers. They should drop pretensions of superiority, reduce social distance from other employees, minimise levels of hierarchy and ensure that pay and benefits differentials are not so large as to be poisonous.

Every enterprise is different

No enterprise will or can combine all the characteristics associated with high achievement. Every enterprise will start from a different point. Some may be cruising along with a strong business model and success in the markets, but need to engage in continuous improvement and innovation to stay in front of the competition. Others may be emerging from a period of near crisis, having suffered the effects of bad strategies. Yet others may be stuck in the past with deeply embedded complacency and resistance to change. The starting points and the processes of moving in a healthy direction will be different for each.

What is needed will be contingent on the nature of the organisation, its strengths and weaknesses, its history and culture and the nature of the 'business'. Pursuing a universal vision of 'good' or copying a template common to all enterprises may result in all kinds of unintended consequences, including throwing the baby of unique excellence out with the bathwater of deficiencies.

Most important, the research findings about high-achieving enterprises do not offer much guidance on what to do to reach the desired state. They do not help much in understanding the here and now, nor do they help to prioritise actions that may bring progress. But given that the research does indicate that high-achieving enterprises have features in common, it must be possible to devise strategies to attain and sustain high achievement.

3. Underpinnings

In the previous chapters, the characteristics of high-achieving enterprises were examined. I observed that while understanding a range of characteristics was useful, it did not give much guidance on what managers can do to reach high achievement. By their actions, managers can build strong and high-achieving enterprises, or they can undermine the foundations that support high achievement. This chapter reviews a range of positive actions – and some destructively negative behaviours.

Building trust and social capital

We are used to being able to place a value on the money and physical assets that are invested in enterprises: their financial capital. And some try to place a value on intellectual capital, as represented by patents and brands, and even more intangibly by know-how and skills locked up in an organisation's staff. It is the latter that can have more worth, because they represent and are responsible for the future value of the enterprise – physical assets, money, brands and patents will all deteriorate in value unless maintained and built upon by an enterprise's human capital.

Recognition of the real value and contribution of people has led to the recognition of what is called social capital, the theory behind which is that relationships matter and that social networks are a valuable asset. Interaction enables people to build communities, to commit themselves to each other, and to knit the social fabric. A sense of belonging and the concrete experience of social networks (and the relationships of trust and tolerance that can be involved) can, it is argued, bring great benefits to people and organisations.

There is now an impressive body of research[1] to show that societies and communities rich in social capital work better in many ways than those that are unequal and divided. Studies into divisions caused by educational and economic inequality show that divided societies with low levels of mutual trust have poorer educational, health, employment, life expectancy and crime records than more equal ones. Research into 'Nordic model' societies that enjoy high trust and social capital indicates that, in addition to other social benefits, they are relatively productive and rich.

Constructive interaction between individuals ultimately becomes a shared set of values and expectations within a community as a whole. Without this interaction, however, trust decays, and eventually this decay begins to manifest itself in serious social and economic problems. The concept of social capital contends that building or rebuilding community and trust requires face-to-face encounters.[2,3]

The same principles apply to enterprises. In the UK, the contrast between the traditional motor industry, which became beset by conflict, and the Japanese-owned motor plants is telling. Nissan's Sunderland plant, which now employs an all-British management and workforce, is among the top rank in productivity and quality. Its success is based on a culture of trust that is underpinned by education, lack of social divisions, involvement and open communication. When Nissan set up the plant, it avoided recruiting staff from the traditional motor industry on the grounds that they were likely to be poisoned by that experience. Rover, the last all-British motor company, collapsed in a welter of recrimination, leaving an unemployed workforce and a small group of managers who had feathered their nests to the tune of more than £40 million. (The same applies to the older parts of the US auto industry. The sight of the CEOs of major US auto companies arriving in private jets to beg money from Congress says it all.)

The old-style Anglo-Saxon industry model involved segregation by employment status, secrecy, low trust levels, conflict and poor productivity and quality. It was, in short, devoid of bonds between top managers and other employees and therefore of social capital. According to Veronica Hope Hailey, a professor at Cass Business School in London:

> Trust is known to be a fundamental enabler of many workplace benefits. If trust levels are high, organisations experience more, and superior, problem-solving and co-operation, a reduced need for constant monitoring and quality checks and increased information sharing. There is also greater acceptance of organisational change initiatives. Fundamentally, research has shown that a sense of high trust between different levels creates a climate of well-being among all people in the workplace with better job satisfaction and greater motivation as beneficial outcomes.

Research by Douglas Kruse[4] and others shows that employee ownership in enterprises works only if it is supported by other practices aimed at enhancing involvement and trust: 'Overall, the results support the idea that workers can gain by sharing ownership, but whether this happens is contingent on other workplace policies.'

Building trusting relationships

Personal contact

The most important facilitators of trust are personal contact, consistency of behaviour, honesty and respect among people. Inevitably, because they are the most visible, the burden of creating and maintaining trust falls most heavily on senior management. Top managers who listen, show respect to others, work with employees to help them solve problems, and impart knowledge and understanding rather than controlling and issuing orders, can also demand high standards and be hard on those who do not try, provided their behaviour is felt to be fair and people respect their skills. The most important attribute for top managers is visibility. Staff generally like to feel that they know their leaders as people and that they can respect them for their competence and values.

Fairness and consistency

Having clear and understandable norms of conduct for the treatment of employees is crucial to maintaining high levels of trust. Organisations can be demanding and tough, provided that they balance demand with support and, especially, behave consistently towards employees at all levels. People may be dismissed for poor performance or dishonesty and this will be accepted by most, provided that they feel decisions are understandable and fair.

High involvement and communication, low social distance

The range of work practices exemplified by Nissan and other high-performance businesses include extensive education, free communication, low-status differentials, work rotation and involvement in improvement. These and other features of the workplaces build high levels of trust across the whole organisation and thus high performance.

Justifiable rewards

There is growing evidence that the huge differentials between top managers and others are creating growing alienation and cynicism among the bulk of employees. In particular, the sense that top managers are the massively rewarded servants of distant uncaring investors is highly undermining.

This book does not set out to solve the problem, but it can be stated that organisations based on a sense of mutuality between employees and directors – and in some cases customers, too – seem to generate a higher sense of loyalty and commitment than those where it is absent. This means that some family companies and smaller organisations with working owners, partnerships like John Lewis, a much admired UK retailer, and organisations based on mutual and co-operative principles may be better places to work and higher achievers than those that create a sense of exploitation.

Aligning stakeholder interests

Research into high achievement reveals that dedication by all to a common cause is a major performance-enhancing factor. Meanwhile, many studies of high-performing organisations of all kinds identify an overriding concern with the quality of the customer experience as a prime characteristic of consistent high achievement. But it is not the only one. Some companies have placed concern for employee well-being at the centre of their value systems; for example, John Lewis was set up with the declared intent of enhancing the well-being and happiness of its partners (employees), and 3M places innovation high on its list of priorities. Johnson & Johnson's 'Credo' (see box) is an excellent example of paying proper respect to the needs of all stakeholders.

What emerges from all this is that the interface between customers and staff lies at the core of high achievement. Staff will treat customers in broadly the same way that their managers treat them. When staff and managers share a commitment to

Johnson & Johnson's Credo

- We believe that our first responsibility is to the doctors, nurses, hospitals, mothers and all others who use our products.

- Our products must always be of the highest quality. We must constantly strive to reduce the cost of these products. Our orders must be promptly and accurately filled.

- Our dealers must make a fair profit.

- Our second responsibility is to those who work with us – the men and women of our plants and offices. They must have a sense of security in their jobs. Wages must be fair and adequate, management just, hours reasonable, and working conditions clean and orderly. Employees should have an organised system for suggestions and complaints.

- Our third responsibility is to our management. Our executives must be people of talent, education, experience and ability. They must be persons of common sense and full understanding.

- Our fourth responsibility is to the communities in which we live. We must be a good citizen – support good works and charity, and bear our fair share of taxes.

- Our fifth and last responsibility is to our stockholders. Business must make a sound profit. Reserves must be created, research must be carried on, adventurous programs developed, and mistakes paid for. Adverse times must be provided for, adequate taxes paid, new machines purchased, new plants built, new products launched, new sales plans developed. We must experiment with new ideas.

- When these things have been done the stockholder must receive a fair return.

customers, it encourages joint problem solving and can remove much of the emotion that can be associated with 'pulling rank'.

Effective and problem strategies

Strategy must embody the organisation's culture – and vice versa

Even if there is no written document describing it, most organisations are pursuing a strategy of some kind – and many pursue several at the same time. The most effective ones are those that are driven by and embody the organisational culture – unless, of course, the culture is rotten. Every organisation of any substance has a history, and during its development it has built up a range of values commonly held by its members. There are also likely to be 'stories' shared by people about significant events or the doings of important people and how certain courses of action led to success or failure. These stories or narratives will, with the values of members, determine in significant ways what the organisation will and will not do and what it will find acceptable or difficult. If all this is added up and mixed with what is measured and what is assumed to be rewarded and punished, it will amount to an informal 'strategy in being'. Further complexity may be added if different parts of the organisation have different values.

Acquisitions usually bring together organisations with different cultures and histories, which often explains long-term underperformance in enterprises that have primarily grown through acquisition rather than organic development. This places the work of corporate planners, investment banking advisers, consultants and top managers in context: they can often be out of touch with the powerful beliefs and assumptions that are embedded deep in the organisations they are working with. What they all too frequently do is create 'synthetic' strategies from their ivory towers, built on numbers and theoretical constructs, which fail because they are not rooted in the realities of the enterprise as a living community.

It is self-evident that when top management is not attuned to its own organisation, it will encounter great difficulty in carrying out any strategy that runs counter to the prevailing narratives and values. Crafting and executing strategy has to be a collaborative activity shared by many staff, including those on the front line.

Henry Mintzberg described the approach to strategy of John Cleghorn, erstwhile CEO of the Bank of Montreal:[5]

> His strategy process appeared to be one of crafting: to foster a flexible structure and open culture, to see the strategic implications of initiatives, and to integrate them with overall vision. That requires his detailed, nuanced knowledge of the organisation.
>
> Of course, this approach, based on rich, grounded information, does not make someone a strategist: that depends on one's capacity for creative synthesis. But I believe that such a style of managing is a prerequisite for developing strategic insights. It is the ability to move between the concrete and the conceptual – not only to understand the specifics but also to be able to generalise creatively about them – that makes a great strategist.
>
> Such is the practice of management as a craft – low key, involved, warm, focused, perhaps quintessentially Canadian. It may not make the headlines, but it seems to work.

Planning and strategy formation as learning

Planning provides rich opportunities for dialogue about the business, competitors, customer needs, and corporate strengths, weaknesses and opportunities. The opportunities for learning can be opened up by adopting a collaborative and exploratory format and style, or closed by making the process threatening and adversarial. The extension of planning processes to involve employees from the top of the organisation to the bottom can enhance learning at every level, especially the most senior – because these are the people most likely to lack personal understanding of customers and competitors. Strategies built on involvement also seem to be easier to enact.

Potentially dangerous strategies

Mergers and acquisitions[6]

Research and experience show that small acquisitions of similar businesses carefully valued and integrated with patience and skill can be a valuable part of a growth strategy[7] – but not the whole strategy, which should have business-building and organic growth as its centrepiece.

The prospect of a big takeover causes more excitement than any other kind of event – apart from a major scandal or corporate failure. A whole industry swings into action to support the deal. Investment banks, financial PR companies, stockbrokers, corporate lawyers and accountants are all there to support or in some cases initiate deals. All earn huge fees from a big transaction. Coming along behind are the consultants who can also make big money helping clients to manage the merged organisation once the deal has been done.

For those on the inside deal-making offers a special buzz. Conceiving and negotiating deals are among the few actions that top managers can execute almost by themselves. There is no need to influence, cajole or network with numerous people to achieve results that will be ascribed to the efforts of many. A big deal can be consummated by a small team: the CEO, the finance director and a few corporate staff, supported by external advisers.

With the thrill of negotiating the deal – planning the conquest, as it were – big acquisitions can take on a life of their own, rather like military campaigns. Advisers often help to sustain the drama by setting up places called 'war rooms' or something similar, from which the general and his troops can plan and execute their campaign.

So, with all the expensive expertise dedicated to delivering the deals, and all the excitement surrounding them, surely

Big mergers are courting disaster

Corporate history is littered with disasters caused by ill-advised mergers. Marconi, AOL Time Warner, Hewlett-Packard, RBS and ABN Amro and thousands of others should be a warning to ambitious leaders and investors alike. But the thrill of the deal seems to overcome rationality.

I worked for two companies that had been seriously affected by mergers. Thorn EMI was created by a merger between Thorn Electrical Industries and EMI. Thorn was a domestic appliances and basic engineering company, strong in the UK and English-speaking countries; EMI was an international advanced electronics and entertainment conglomerate. The cultures of the two 'partners' were radically different, as were their business models. The mess created by this gigantic merger, which was initiated in 1980 and resulted in a string of sales at a loss and a demerger in 1992, was finally brought to a conclusion when a much diminished EMI Music was sold to a competitor in 2012. Along the way, the destruction of value was huge.

Redland, a leading international construction materials company, indulged in a series of major acquisitions through the 1980s and into the 1990s. Unfortunately, most of the

M&A activity is one of the best ways of creating strategic value. Or is it? Apparently not, as in 2003 the US National Bureau of Economic Research reported:[8]

> Mergers and acquisitions destroy shareholder wealth in the acquiring companies. New research from the NBER shows that, over the past 20 years, US takeovers have led to (net) losses of more than $200 billion for shareholders. However, this result is dominated by the big losses experienced by shareholders in big companies.

acquisitions were overpriced and the acquired companies poorly integrated, which resulted in an estimated destruction of value amounting to more than £2 billion. That burden eventually brought Redland down and it was acquired by an international competitor.

I will end this sorry tale with another example from an article in the *Observer* on February 16, 2003. Under the heading, 'Invensys mergers turn to dross', the correspondent says:

> Two out of three mergers fail to create value. And if anyone doubts this they should ask shareholders in Invensys, the company with the crazy name and crazy strategy. The engineering and controls firm has spent years building up its empire only to offload vast chunks of it along the way when hindsight invariably struck ... On Friday Invensys's shares slumped by 53% after warning its second half figures would be 25% below those of the previous six months. They are now worth just 19p, a sixth of what they were valued at a year ago. In Invensys's sorry case, the whole is really less than the sum of its parts.

There is evidence that more than 50 per cent of big mergers fail to create value. The reasons are complex, but a few stand out:

- Merging organisations is a social process, and as the social fabrics of the merging organisations are likely to be very different, the disruption caused can last for decades.

- Most large acquisitions are based on a theoretical notion of 'synergy'. But real synergy can be assessed only through a detailed understanding of what organisations are doing at operational levels – in particular, how they interface with customers, how they make and design products, and how information is transmitted and used.

■ This is often disguised by adopting a purely financial definition of synergy, regarding it as the amount of cost saved through getting rid of duplication and people. Realising real synergy requires close collaboration between a lot of people in the acquiring and acquired enterprises. What happens too often is demonstrations of dominance on the part of many people in the acquirer and resentment or withdrawal among those in the acquired – certainly not the climate for close collaboration between equals.

■ The surface manifestations of M&A failure are financial, in particular miscalculating synergy benefits and getting the price wrong. Often the sheer thrill of the chase can cause top managers, abetted by advisers, to get carried away and end up paying more than the target is worth to them.

'Financialisation'

It started with large companies that are quoted in the stock market. According to a research study conducted by the CRESC in 2006, the essence of corporate strategy in Anglo-Saxon economies has changed over some twenty-five years. This is the period when institutional investors' influence on companies increased considerably and led to the present position where managers believe that their tenure, reputation and wealth are mainly dependent on pleasing these investors.[9] An effect of the growing dominance of the markets has been a change in the nature and substance of corporate strategy. In the 1980s strategy was concerned with competing in the markets for customers: corporations were assumed to be players in an industry setting seeking sources of competitive advantage over rivals for the same customers. Now, according to the CRESC, corporate strategy is much more concerned with creating and communicating 'narratives' that will please investors. In *Financialization and Strategy, Narrative and Numbers*,[10] Julie Froud, a professor and director of postgraduate programmes at the University of Manchester, and her colleagues examine the nature of corporate narratives and reveal that many of them have little to do with what enterprises actually do. But they also point out that the top management of large quoted enterprises have become fixated on serving the needs of the stock markets and associated governance institutions.

Building or undermining organisations

Building healthy, open, learning organisations

For learning to be an organisation-wide phenomenon, certain important conditions need to be met. Organisations must be valued as human institutions that have a communal life and distinctive culture, and can harbour a sense of destiny. This is a far cry from commonly held notions of organisations as machines or as collections of assets that can be manipulated, bought and sold. Machines and assets do not learn – in fact they do not generate value unless activated by human ingenuity and skill. Therefore for an enterprise to have a future, its organisation needs to be treated as the organism that carries the current and future business. This means motivating and encouraging people to give of their best and to learn continuously.

Organisations designed for purpose

Organisational design is discussed in Part 2. For the time being, it is sufficient to say that there is no standard form of organisation. There are two factors that cause differences:

■ The nature of the business or industry. Some industries have highly dispersed customers with considerable local or regional differences in culture or taste. Therefore it is sensible to devolve a considerable degree of discretion in such issues as product mix and pricing. In other industries, technology and more uniform customer needs may suit a more centralised design.

■ The context of the business. An enterprise in relatively stable markets with a sound business model can devolve more to the front line than one in crisis. When problems occur that may threaten the existence of the enterprise it may be necessary to centralise decision-making until the crisis is overcome.

Supporting a learning environment

Top managers must choose between favouring 'stick and carrot' and coercion and supporting learning and encouragement. Unfortunately, in the modern world, there are many examples of leaders who have chosen diktat and coercion as their favoured tactics – and there is an undercurrent of approval from investors and the business media for 'toughness' and hard driving as chosen styles. But there is little evidence that driving people remorselessly creates lasting high achievement.

A better approach lies in using learning as a major tool for improvement. This means using every opportunity to foster learning and exploration, through both formal employee development and, equally importantly, building learning into the routines of organisational life. There is a close connection between organisational cohesion and learning and innovation and adaptability. The best learning is that which is shared and passed around the organisation. Learning should not be confined to particular levels of seniority or functions. There is a place for external training programmes, especially for developing specialist knowledge and skills. But the best form of learning is likely to be internally sourced and managed. It is also likely to bring together people from many levels and functions, so that there is a sharing of perspectives and views of the world.

Allowing free flow of information

André de Waal's research chimes with my experience in that it finds that high-achieving enterprises are concerned to ensure that all staff feed off a common base of information. They also concentrate on enabling free flows of information and learning. Nissan follows a 'seventy percent' rule, which means that 70 per cent or more of all information is freely shared across the whole organisation.

Allowing 'slack' time for exploration and experimentation

Most enterprises that have been rated as inventive allow time and support to enable people to try new things and follow projects of their own in the belief that the results will be worthwhile.

Being demanding and supportive

Long time horizons should not be used as an excuse for enterprises to get off the hook of high achievement and lapse into quiet torpor. Leaders should always demand high performance and keep expectations high for the whole organisation. Bill Yearsley, former CEO of Redland North America and now a professor at the University of Colorado, developed a motto: 'Give freedom, expect results.' His behaviour as a manager was a potent mix of high demands: on the organisation that he led and particularly on his direct reports, who knew that he sometimes had a lashing tongue. But he was considered to be consistent and fair. He gave praise where it was due and insisted that everyone in the organisation spent ample time and energy on learning and improvement. Yearsley made sure that his requirements for people to learn were taken seriously by investing in individual and group development programmes and by being seen to be pursuing his own development. The combination of high demand and high support created a culture that enabled the organisation he led to become a top performer in its industry and a generator of internal talent for developing the business.

Making organisational politics a force for good

Every organisation has politics, because every organisation is a place where power is deployed, where people may have differing views about important issues and decisions, and where people will seek to influence outcomes. This is a pretty good description of a 'politics-rich' environment. I believe that politics are inevitable, and there are 'good' and 'bad' politics. My definition of bad politics is power or influence used to further personal interests or drive through decisions based on power plays, regardless of the wider and longer-term interests of an organisation. Good politics is influence or power used to further the interests of the organisation.

It is crucial that healthy politics is practised from the top, because then it will pervade the whole organisation.

Destructive forces

Insularity, complacency and remoteness

There is a large body of evidence showing that managements can become insular and stuck, even arrogant, if they are lulled into a sense of invulnerability by success or simply ignorance and complacency.

Problems arise when top managers become inward-looking and are cut off from their customers and staff. Close-knit cadres of top managers, strongly bonded by long association with or affiliation to strong leaders, can develop a resistance to feedback from the organisation. This can result in a pattern of thinking described as 'groupthink', which can cause all manner of inappropriate behaviour, ranging from wild corporate escapades to complacent inertia.

Some managers become cut off from their own organisations by identifying too closely with the financial markets or some other powerful external forces. They may never achieve real connections with staff and customers because they are not there long enough – or they may believe that an 'upward and outward' focus is best for the business or for their own reputations. Similar kinds of behaviour can be manifested by middle managers who become alienated from senior colleagues.

EMI Records UK, once a well-known music company, had eleven managing directors in twelve years up to 1990 and became immune to new top managers until the arrival of one who stayed for more than seven years. As the last 'newcomer' was also competent, the positive effect on performance was dramatic. EMI's progress since has been less happy, and after a period in private equity hands the company was bought by Universal.

Fear and conflict

Many organisations are frightening places to work. Bullying and harassment are common in some industries, the financial services sector reportedly one of the worst. The popular media lionises people who are capable of striking fear in the minds of others. Some top managers cultivate frightening personas and initiate reigns of terror. The much-revered Jack Welch was described by a former colleague whose business was acquired by GE as a very frightening man, who sat at the back of a meeting in which he was making a presentation, from time to time shouting 'Bullshit'.

Alan Sugar, a wealthy British businessman, has become a popular TV personality through his programme *The Apprentice*. His catchphrase is 'You're fired'. The programme seems to encourage the apprentices to compete and undermine each other. Such behaviours are seldom hallmarks of high-achieving enterprises.

Insufficient or excessive performance expectations

Organisations are not inexhaustible machines. They can be driven too hard or left to languish in inefficient sloth. They can also be underfed and deprived of intellectual challenge and stimulation. For each organisation, there is a 'zone of optimal performance'. Drive it too hard to overachieve, and it will eventually flag and deteriorate.

But it is also possible to let organisations grow fat and happy, and not stimulate them sufficiently. The effects of slack management and poor practices are equally catastrophic. Eventually, such organisations will fail to satisfy customers or make insufficient returns to sustain the business.

Initiative overload

People who have not worked in the boiler-houses of organisations and experienced what it takes to make positive change take root are not in a position to impose programmes of transformatory change. A common cause of confusion and unintended consequences is pressure by impatient and distant leaders or external stakeholders who want change and want it quickly. Often, they issue a constant flow of ordinances, targets and diktats, not waiting for the impact of one set of initiatives to become clear before embarking on another round of change.

Pulling it all together: managing effectively from the boardroom to the front line

High-achieving enterprises are organised in such a way that there are effectively two-way connections between those who make corporate-level decisions through to the 'front line' of employees who make products and serve customers. If these connections fail, the organisation will suffer from potentially serious malfunctions – especially if top managers become cut off from the reality of their own organisations and the bulk of people are left to speculate on what 'they' are up to.

The fundamental role of the board

The paramount responsibility of the board must be to clearly articulate and be guardians of the fundamental values that underpin everything that the enterprise does. These include:

- the rights of stakeholders and the priority given to their interests;
- managing succession to senior roles;
- the treatment of staff;
- ethical standards in relation to society and dealing with customers or clients;

■ learning and innovation;

■ investment and preserving long-term corporate health and vitality.

Any enterprise that seals its boundaries from the external environment is likely to be dysfunctional. Most enterprises will send out and receive signals from their surrounding environments. The most successful are well attuned to what is happening with customers, competitors and suppliers, and owners and investors. Most will also seek to influence external influencers.

Keeping abreast of environmental threats and opportunities will almost certainly require senior managers to use all the organisation's antennae, especially those of people who are in touch with customers. Effective organisations use all their senses and seek to intelligently balance responses to signals from all significant stakeholders.

Effective boards

Most enterprises have a body responsible for governance and strategy. In some cases, the board of directors may be the executive team. In larger quoted companies, investors insist that boards include external directors to represent their interests. And some enterprises voluntarily invite people with experience and wisdom to sit on their boards.

Over the last three decades or so, the pressures on public company boards to ensure good corporate governance have grown exponentially, driven by governments and investment institutions. These pressures have been fuelled by what might be described as 'institutionalised mistrust', which has become enshrined in the Corporate Auditing Accountability and Responsibility Act (Sarbanes-Oxley) in the US and the UK Corporate Governance Code.

The trouble is that – despite the travails of Enron, Tyco and WorldCom – evidence shows that by far the most value in companies is destroyed by inept strategic leadership rather than dishonesty.[11] On both sides of the Atlantic, boards have been supine or have supported outrageous strategic blunders – such as those that supported the mergers of AOL and Time Warner, RBS and ABN Amro, and Daimler and Chrysler. But worst of all, I wonder what the boards of the banks and insurance companies that nearly brought the world economy to its knees by their venal and irresponsible behaviour thought they were doing? Many companies have been damaged, even crippled, by faulty strategies and appalling leadership while their boards have seemingly just watched or even cheered from the sidelines.

The reasons for this state of affairs are legion. My research with John Roberts of Judge Business School, University of Cambridge,[12] revealed that the very governance pressures that are supposed to make boards effective are actually felt to be driving fissures between executive and non-executive directors and undermining the strategic contributions of non-executive directors. There are many other potential problems, including unwillingness to challenge, a lack of informed critique by non-executives, excessive sensitivity to media and investor pressures, and a lack of time spent by busy non-executives. It can be the case that boards containing too many members of the 'great and good' are rendered ineffectual by the egos and sensitivities of board members.

Rather than dwell on the negatives, here are some indicators of potential board effectiveness, starting with the board as a de facto top team. Effective top teams are likely to:

- have dealt effectively with issues of power and influence so that no individual or subgroup dominates;
- have appropriate membership for the needs of the time and context;
- have clear and orderly working methods;
- critique their own decisions and team effectiveness;
- avoid inward-looking perspectives and groupthink;

- be clear about their roles and contacts in the wider organisation.

Some boards will contain a mix of internal executive and external non-executive directors. This can make the board's processes more complex. From direct experience and my research with Roberts, high-achieving boards will demonstrate the following characteristics:

- They know their limitations, and do not attempt to create strategy or perform executive tasks. Realistic boards will understand that their best role is to question, add wisdom to, modify, support – or in extreme cases, reject – strategic proposals delivered through the organisation.

- They can flex their membership to bring in appropriate experience for the strategic context.

- They are well-informed about all facets of a business and can bring appropriate special skills to bear for important decisions.

- They regard stewardship of the enterprise as their primary purpose, and will not allow pressures from external agencies to deflect their dedication to its long-term health.

- They stay closely in touch with the business and keep up to date with changes in the business environment, but exercise skilful judgements about when and how they intervene.

- The non-executive members will detect and pick up on fissures and souring relationships between executive directors. They will keep in touch with the quality of relationships between the board and the wider organisation.

- They will take a direct interest in non-financial issues, particularly key appointments, staff development, succession and key competencies.

- Directors will have respect for each other and there will be an atmosphere of trust leading to the possibility of open and vigorous debate. They will not allow formality or power distance to get in the way of open, relaxed relationships.

- They will ensure that important issues of governance are managed in a way that does not detract from the board's strategic role.

- Non-executive directors led by the chair will view their primary role as adding experience and expertise to the work of the board and mentoring executives.

Effective executive managers

I have known and worked for many chief executives, managing directors and other general managers. A few were truly effective – they knew their business and people, and they were demanding, questioning, active networkers, good listeners, communicative and when needed supportive givers of good advice. Most were not as effective. The commonest malaise was creating barriers through status and privileges. But several had not made a successful transition from a specialist (usually finance) role. Some were extremely defensive, not tolerating critique or deprecating humour. The worst could be described as critical, looking for fault, punitive and rather secretive. They often had offices guarded by more than one secretary. The very worst were suffering from what Lord Acton observed: power tends to corrupt and absolute power corrupts absolutely.

The more effective ones were more concerned with the success of the enterprise than personal status.

Given the vast range of different contexts, is it possible to capture some factors that differentiate and set apart high-achieving managers? John Kotter's research for his book *The General Managers* demonstrates that there are a number of key determinants that distinguish the most effective ones from others:

▪ **Personal characteristics.** These include a high level of ambition, stamina, and a desire to achieve and exercise power to get things done. High achievers share temperamental evenness and optimism, an ability to think and synthesise different kinds of information to make sense of complexity, and high interpersonal skills, together with a detailed knowledge of the business and organisation they are in – and in particular, the ability to form many co-operative relationships with other people in the business and their own organisation. These characteristics are developed throughout life and honed from early years through whole careers.

▪ **What they do – networking and agenda-setting.** Initially (on taking up a job), they use their interpersonal skills to create networks of co-operative relationships with all those who are important to success in the job. The information generated by these relationships enables them to create 'agendas' defining important issues to be addressed. They do so using a continuous, incremental, largely informal process of discussions and dialogue using many subtle methods. They get their networks to implement their agendas by directly and indirectly influencing other people. They spend most of their time with others (including peers, outsiders, bosses, other directors and particularly subordinates at many levels) discussing a wide range of subjects in short and disjointed conversations that are often not planned in advance, in which the leaders ask a lot of questions and rarely give direct orders.

▪ **Why do they behave like this?** Because of the nature of senior executive jobs, which require: (1) decision-making in an environment characterised by uncertainty, great diversity, containing an enormous amount of potentially relevant information; and (2) implementation through a large and diverse group of subordinates, peers, bosses and outsiders. Often, they have partial or limited control over the networks of people they need to influence to get things done.

Maybe the final word should rest with another astute observer of management in action. Henry Mintzberg is much more impressed by what he describes as 'managing quietly' than the posturings of charismatic leaders. He says:[13]

> Quiet managers care for their organisation; they do not slice away problems as surgeons do. They spend more time preventing problems than fixing them, because they know enough to know when and how to intervene. In a sense, it is more like natural medicine, the prescription of small doses to stimulate the system to heal itself. Better still, it is more like nursing, gentle care that, in itself, becomes cure … Quiet managing is about infusion, change that seeps in slowly, profoundly. Rather than having change thrust upon them in dramatic, superficial episodes, everyone takes responsibility for making sure that serious changes take hold. This does not mean changing everything all the time – which is another way of saying anarchy. It means always changing some things while holding most others steady. Call this natural continuous improvement, if you like. The trick, of course, is to know what to change when. And to achieve that there is no substitute for a leadership with an intimate understanding of the organisation working with a workforce that is respected and trusted. That way, when people leave, including the leaders, progress continues.

Effective corporate offices

Corporate offices come under a number of guises: headquarters, head office, office of the CEO and in one French company *siège*, which means seat or throne. All these titles seem to imply that somehow the corporate office is a mixture of royal palace and brain of the company. Some writers have asserted that the board and corporate office do indeed represent the central intellect that drives and controls enterprises. But many dispute this, contending that knowledge and wisdom are widely dispersed in most enterprises of any size.

The difference between the world of the corporate headquarters and that of the manufacturing plant or sales office can best be characterised as that between a world where nothing is tangible and information is a synthetic representation of reality, and a place where it is possible to see, feel, hear and smell the substance of the real world. In other words, it is the difference between playing virtual wars on a computer and actually being among the explosions, death and injury in a world where real bullets fly.

Unless they make a real effort of will, corporate managers can be trapped into dependence on reports, numbers and plans on computers or in manuals – generally information that has been through a series of syntheses.

Corporate office roles are as follows:

- Most larger organisations will have a range of statutory, legal and financial obligations. In a typical company quoted on the stock market, there are obligations about the provision of information to the regulatory authorities and investment institutions. These tasks are normally carried out by the legal, finance and investor relations functions in liaison as necessary with the chief executive and chair, who may have specific legal responsibilities. Most large companies quoted on stock markets go to elaborate lengths to manage their relationships with investors and the media, because it is known that both will have a critical impact on the support the company and its top managers receive and thus on their reputations, tenure and wealth.

- The corporate office usually supports the board in pursuing its strategic and governance roles. It is also generally the support organisation for the management functions of the chief executive. Activities include managing the planning processes, performance management, and the provision and consolidation of financial and management information.

■ Corporate functions such as finance, public affairs, human resources and strategic planning are normally embedded in corporate offices, often with (excessively) large support departments.

■ Maybe most important is the role of the corporate office in managing the deployment of resources, which normally means capital allocation and the development and deployment of people.

■ Last and most problematic are the support roles of corporate managers for the operating entities of the enterprise. In his book *Imaginization*,[14] Gareth Morgan characterises an important part of this role as akin to that of a bumblebee, moving from flower to flower and spreading pollen. Corporate staff should justify their existence by helping managers across the organisation to add value.

A director of ABF (Associated British Foods), a huge family-controlled business, described the roles of its corporate staff succinctly:

> We practice high engagement – the small number of people in the corporate centre travel incessantly and maintain close personal contact with those who run the operating companies. Taken together, these are the key people in our company. We strongly believe in 'getting mud on our boots': so corporate staff not only travel to subsidiaries' offices, they get out into the field to see where it really happens. This mode strongly challenges corporate managers to be relevant and be able to add value to the operations. There is no place to hide in the corporate office.

The roles of middle management

Between the corporate apex and the front line of most large enterprises lies the middle of the organisation. It falls on middle management to integrate the range of functions and specialisms that are needed to create and provide the enterprise's products or services.

Communication

Middle managers have to interpret the wishes of top managers and turn them into programmes of action that will achieve the desired results. They are therefore in a critical position: they can communicate important messages from the front line to the top and also interpret what top management require and make these wishes practical to and achievable by the front line. Middle managers can make or break enterprises. If they play politics and bend or twist information for political or power play purposes, they can cripple an enterprise. Conversely, they can help make it work as a coherent and purposeful community.

Managing the front line

As well as making the organisation work smoothly, middle managers have the key role of managing the front line. In a typical manufacturing organisation, middle managers are responsible for development, production engineering, manufacturing, sales and service activities. In addition to managing their own departments efficiently, they are involved in making sure that these activities are sufficiently integrated to produce a good result for customers.

In service and financial businesses, middle managers have the crucial role of motivating sales forces and servicing frontline staff, while ensuring that ethical and quality standards are maintained. Top managers are too far from the customer interfaces to manage the front line. Many of the recent issues affecting banking and other service businesses are the result of middle management problems.

Integrating key activities

As an example, huge problems of poor quality and delivery in a technical products organisation were not solved until middle managers responsible for engineering, manufacturing and sales were formed into teams and given direct responsibility for specifying, designing, engineering, manufacturing and delivering products. Previous attempts from the top to control these processes by devising procedures to solve relationship problems had failed miserably.

Nurseries for top management talent

High-achieving organisations show a strong tendency to nurture and develop their own talent, so that there is a common thread of experience and understanding running through the organisation. Unfortunately, the process of 'financialisation', together with the growing dominance of financial and business school types, has seriously undermined the values, skills and deep understanding that come from working through an organisation before reaching the top. Most accountants and business school graduates are not naturally endowed with such rich experience, and far too many of them seem to assume that whole swathes of experience can be sidestepped without damage.

The front line

Japanese practices emphasise the crucial roles of those at the front line who make and sell an enterprise's products or services. They also emphasise engaging frontline people intimately in the processes of innovation and improvement that keep quality and efficiency advancing continuously. Just in time and lean manufacturing practices together with total quality management and quality circles, all of which originated in Japan, have been widely adopted on both sides of the Atlantic. The Nissan factory in Sunderland in the UK is run on Japanese principles modified for the UK environment. Features of the Nissan approach are as follows:

■ The absence of formal status divisions as expressed through different styles of dress or differentiation of offices.

Managers are expected to behave as colleagues to other staff, not as controllers.

■ Training that emphasises the importance of a common understanding of the dynamics of the business among all staff, so that all can appreciate key performance data fully. The rule of thumb is that frontline and top managers should share at least 70 per cent of common business understanding and skill, in addition to the requirements of their specialisms.

■ All staff feed off the same information sources – there is little information withheld about performance and plans.

The results have been impressive. Nissan's Sunderland plant is one of the most productive in the world, in contrast to the often miserable performance of British owned and managed plants, most of which are now defunct. Nissan's experiences give the lie to the idea that organisations can function effectively where there are inappropriately large differences in status, rewards and roles between the top and the front line. Most successful enterprises take an integrative approach and encourage contact, communication and bonding between staff at all levels.

Making it all work well requires human contact

Ian Pringle, erstwhile HR director and then joint CEO of TDG, a logistics company, is definite about the most important factor that will affect whether enterprises are successful. He says: 'All the sophisticated planning and performance management systems in the world, supporting the best strategies, will count for nought unless the people at the front line are clear about what is meant by a good performance and understand how their contributions line up with corporate goals.' He illustrates this by drawing a person, surrounded by vastly complex systems, processes and policies. 'Unless this man or woman clearly understands what they have to do to help the organisation be successful, all the surrounding "stuff" is worse than useless …

"Helping them understand" is a human process, transmitted through people, not procedures.'

Management theorists have devised systems and processes of incredible complexity to automate the processes of strategy formation, planning and performance management. There is little evidence that these and the supporting hierarchies of metrics have made a real contribution to performance.

But those observers and commentators on management who have taken the trouble to observe good management in action have revealed a different world of informal relationships, conversations and dialogues making up networks of mutual understanding among people at various organisational levels. In its early days Hewlett-Packard developed the idea of MBWA or 'management by walking about', which vividly describes an informal style that can reduce the barriers between different functions and levels in organisations. In this way many staff get to know top managers as real people, not disembodied beings protected by secretaries, big offices, chauffeur-driven limousines or corporate jets. And in turn, top managers become well-informed about what is really going on at the front line and with customers and competitors.

It is most important to realise that the structures of authority, communications and relationships described above take time to build and are among the first things to be damaged by insensitive 'top down' reorganisations. Most organisations work because of informal understandings that will invariably be invisible to isolated senior managers or outsiders.

Actions that speak louder than words

Collaborative planning

Forward planning should be a collaborative exercise between corporate and operational managers. Far too often planning becomes formalised and fragmented, encouraging elaborate game playing. One large organisation dispensed with formal presentations of divisional plans and instead involved corporate and divisional managers working together to create them. The process involved joint pre-preparation by staff managers. Each year there was a three-day meeting of divisional and corporate top managers to thrash out and agree the plans and outline budgets, which were then finalised by the staff managers. In this way, trust was built and corporate managers were challenged to add value to divisional thinking. But most importantly, there was informal mutual understanding about risks and opportunities, so that the organisation could respond quickly to events and problems as they arose.

Encouraging information interchange

Many organisations allow barriers to develop between different parts and functions, thus making communication and mutual understanding difficult. Some overcome this problem by making it a practice for staff in different parts to interchange with others. In particular, requiring corporate office senior staff to work for two or three weeks in jobs at the front line each year keeps them in touch with reality and helps them to appreciate the skills and importance of frontline staff.

Nor should interchanges be restricted to senior managers. This practice can work well for secretaries and personal assistants, who in most organisations are an important source of communication and can lubricate the wheels of commerce. A regular programme of exchanges can work wonders for relationships and understanding.

Getting career structures right

Sustainably high-achieving enterprises often grow their own talent. Ensuring that top managers do not reach their elevated positions unless they have worked their way through the ranks from the front line to the board guarantees a sound understanding of the business from top to bottom. Some would argue strongly that enterprises must bring in new blood from outside. But internally grown talent can be kept fresh by means of regular secondments to other organisations and introducing external perspectives through development programmes.

Contemporary experience indicates that leaders without a well-developed picture of how organisations work and their people and functions interrelate will devise changes that cause chaos because the effects on people at different levels have not been properly taken into account. Impatient politicians hell-bent on modernising are among the worst offenders.

Team projects and joint problem solving

Setting up project teams with members drawn from different parts and different levels of the organisation is usually a much better way of tackling difficult problems than hiring expensive consultants. Leavening project teams with external skills can ensure that the requisite skills are deployed and, most importantly, that the learning generated by the project stays inside the enterprise. The knee-jerk tendency to call for consultants at the first sign of problems can be wasteful in money and knowledge. And bringing together skills from different parts of the enterprise is of course a major integrative opportunity.

Making top managers human and accessible

Many of the trappings of corporate power – large offices, special travel arrangements and praetorian guards of staff and secretaries – are expensive and unnecessary. Top managers' time may be valuable, but not so precious to merit corporate jets when there are airlines. We tend to overestimate the contributions of high-profile individuals. Most high achievement comes from a fusion of the efforts of many people, and an obsession with a few individuals can actually undermine performance. Deliberately dismantling the trappings of status and power can be hugely liberating and also exposes top managers to the need to be demonstrably competent when working alongside junior colleagues.

The seventy per cent rule

There is strong evidence, reported by André de Waal and referred to earlier, that high-achieving organisations are open about key business data and that all staff feed off a common information system. While there are some matters that cannot be shared with all staff in their entirety, such as financial market-sensitive information in the case of quoted companies, it still seems strange that external investors should have special privileges over staff, when it is the staff who create the profits.

For enterprises not constrained in this way, the key is to educate the whole workforce to a common basis of understanding of the business, so that most performance-related information can be shared and understood. Nissan ensures that at least 70 per cent of all information is shared commonly from the top to the front line of the organisation.

Devolving responsibility and creating whole jobs

The concept of shareholder value may have been found wanting, but a constructive variant for measuring performance that has been tried involves assessing the capital deployed in each of an organisation's businesses. Managers were rewarded for improving the cash generated for each quantum of capital deployed. The rewards were financial, but more importantly managers were able to retain some of the increased cash flow for improvement and growth projects for their businesses. Said one manager:

> I have always had responsibility for staff and customer relations, but now I can have a measure of control over investment, I feel at last like I am running a complete business. Before, corporate managers took away all the cash my business generated and I believe wasted a lot of it. Now I can deploy capital better than them, because I understand my business and its opportunities and risks better than head office.

Dilbert and Scott Adams understand this.

Knowledge and resources

What managers need to know

Introduction

The world of business and enterprise is complex and ever-changing. Organisations have to adapt to changing circumstances and deal with a plethora of pressures and opportunities. Managers have to be able to 'read' signals from the environment around them. Some of these signals will be strong and may denote a need for urgent action. Others may be fainter and may be early warnings of changes to come. They will need to be monitored but perhaps not acted on immediately.

Managers also need to understand the strengths and weaknesses of their own organisations and be able to compare these with competitors or other organisations that could provide them with services. They need to assess the competences of important people and teams – and make judgements about the capacity of their enterprises to respond to challenges and achieve short- and longer-term goals.

Most importantly, effective managers understand how to motivate people and steer whole organisations in desired directions. They need to perform these roles through networks of colleagues at many levels and in many specialisms, using the power of persuasion to get people 'on side' with their agendas.

There will be times when disagreements will occur; when some people may not feel that their interests are being served by the direction of travel of the organisation. Powerful individuals may have different interests and pursue different agendas. Those directing enterprises must be adept at recognising resistance and knowing where it is coming from and what to do about it. In other words, they will have to be skilled at playing politics.

It will become evident from this description of organisational life that a sound grasp of accounting and finance is not enough to enable managers to negotiate the complex and changing worlds inside and outside their enterprises. But in the contemporary world, there seems to be an excessive reliance on synthetic numerical information, which can present a distorted and too often inaccurate picture of the complex realities of the world. When asked why his company did not have a qualified accountant on the board, Bertrand Collomb, erstwhile president of Lafarge, a French construction materials company, said: 'Accounting is not a strategic issue.'

So the truth is that managers will need to understand and deal with the world around them through a number of 'lenses'. Maybe the more important ones will provide a view of the behaviour of people, as individuals and in groups and communities, because the organised skills and activities of people are the only living part of any enterprise. That is what creates value.

This part of the book provides guidance to understanding several important facets of the life of enterprises, in particular:

- economic performance

- the contribution of the social sciences

- psychology

- politics and power.

4. Economic performance

This chapter develops frameworks and ideas about how the economic performance of enterprises can be understood and assessed. The intention is to demonstrate that simply assessing the success of an enterprise through narrow financial lenses is likely to give a misleading picture.

The current age has seen a rise of faith in the use of metrics. Financial metrics are the lingua franca of the banking and investment sectors. In the Anglo-Saxon countries, there are many more accountants per head than in most other nations. The UK leads the way: it is estimated that almost half of all accountants in the developed world are British. The US follows, but also majors in lawyers. In the past forty years or so there has been a rise in faith in the veracity of numbers and synthesised performance data. Politicians bandy statistics like swords, seemingly able to present different perspectives on the same phenomena through massaging or selecting the numbers to suit the message.

I contend that an obsession with concrete, numerical information can lead to gross errors of judgement. 'The numbers' may indicate that something is right or wrong in an enterprise, but they are unlikely to give much clue as to why, and certainly almost nothing about how to sustain success or rectify problems. They are inadequate for predicting future performance. All this requires different frames of understanding. But in deference to the prevailing fashions, I will start with finance and 'numbers'.

Measuring financial performance

Accounting measures such as profit and loss

Many years ago, the American Association of Accountants published a monograph entitled *Impediments to the use of Management Information*. Its contents are summarised below.

Ideally, the performance measures that managers monitor and use for management decision-making should go up when economic value is created and down when economic value is destroyed. But short-term profit measures and accounting returns often do not do that. This has been shown consistently in research over various periods.

This low correlation should not come as a surprise. Many things affect accounting profits but not economic values, and vice versa:

■ While value is future-oriented, accounting profit measures focus on the past. Future revenues, and most future expenses, are not anticipated.

■ Accounting systems are transactions-oriented. Although fair value accounting attempts to capture changes in the value of certain assets recorded on the balance sheet, many changes in value are not captured in profit figures.

■ Accounting measurement rules are conservatively biased. They are slow to recognise gains and revenues but quick to recognise expenses and losses.

- Accounting rules ignore some economic values and value changes that cannot be measured accurately and objectively with conventional accounting measures. Prime examples are investments designed to create intangible assets, such as brand, reputation and employee skills.

- Accounting profit measures ignore the cost of equity capital, which is usually much more significant than the cost of debt capital.

- Accounting profit measures ignore risk and changes in risk.

So, are there better means of understanding financial performance?

Value creation[1]

Moving the spotlight from measures such as profit or income to the creation of value can transform the ways in which we think about financial success. It enables us to think of the creation of value as a cyclical activity that occurs over a long period of time. Value creation requires investment on many dimensions. Simply extracting money will eventually decrease the value of an enterprise. Too much focus on cost can degrade the capacity of staff and in turn the quality and value of their outputs to customers and clients.

Value creation measures

Measures are primarily focused on whether the enterprise is generating sufficient value to satisfy the expectations of its suppliers of capital, which may be in the form of borrowings or equity capital raised in the financial markets. The use of the stock-market price as an indicator of value creation doesn't work because of the volatility and short-term orientation of stock markets, resulting in changes in the value of companies that have little to do with their performance.

Many take the view that the best means of assessing financial performance is to use the generation of cash as the fundamental measure, because it is more difficult to manipulate than profit. Cash value added is assessed by determining whether the enterprise is generating sufficient cash over time to:

- provide satisfactory returns for investors;

- cover the costs of maintaining the existing business;

- invest enough in people, products and innovation to secure the future.

In this case, value creation means generating sufficient cash flow over relatively long time frames to fund essential maintenance and development expenditure, pay taxes, and repay the cost of the capital and cash invested in the business.

To make this work, it is necessary to value a business in terms of the capital invested in it at a point in time. For companies quoted on stock markets, capital can be expressed as the long-term value of shareholder equity plus borrowings. The capital invested in divisions will have to be calculated for each, using an estimate of the capital invested to form a baseline. Then the relationship between cash generation and the value of capital can be determined, as can the weighted cost of that capital, using external or actual measures. For most companies, the cost of capital will be about 10 per cent of its value.

Each year, the value of extra capital investment can be added to the original figure and divestment of capital subtracted. The aim is to maintain returns over time above the cost of capital – this represents the financial value created. This has been a successful approach to enlarging the roles of division and business unit managers, especially if they are allowed to reinvest a proportion of the value created in their businesses rather than holding that responsibility with a distant corporate office.

Human asset accounting

The dominance of financial accounting and its strong tendency to regard people as a cost – therefore to be minimised – has led to attempts to place a value on people at work.

I am sceptical about the value of human asset accounting. There are too many variables and imponderables attached to the performance of people at work. Furthermore, attempting to use accounting methods smacks of playing to a financial audience that places little value on intangibles.

But much effort has been put into trying to measure the value of people. Rensis Likert, founder of the University of Michigan's Institute for Social Research, posed the following question:

> Suppose that tomorrow all the jobs are empty, but you still have available all the rest of the resources: buildings, factories, industrial plants, patents, stocks, money, and so on; except, of course, for the personnel. How much time would it take you to recruit the necessary personnel, train it until they are able to assume all the existing functions at the present competitive level and integrate it in the organisation in the same way they now are?

This may raise interesting issues but ultimately leads us up a blind alley. The fact is that an enterprise without people is a museum of rapidly depreciating assets. Likert's company would have gone bust long before it managed to find a new crew.

But there is merit in being sensibly aware of the costs involved in employment. It is relatively easy to account for the costs of employing people and to measure their efficiency. It is also useful to think in terms of opportunity costs. Abuse and exploitation will eventually tell in lost performance, and losing valuable staff will have consequences that range from damaging to fatal. Replacement costs can also be accounted for, as indicated by this extract from Bola Agbonile's human resources website:

> If a person's salary is X, their true value to the firm is probably X times 2.5 when we take into account their replacement

costs, training/embedding in of replacements, pressure on remaining staff who have to cover, lost production and loss of their networks. Lose a good player and who will replace them? How much time will pass before the organisation regains their know-how and drive?

If measures of people value are to be sought, there may be more virtue in assessing the value of everything except people – money, physical assets like buildings, and intellectual property tied up in product and patents – and then depreciating them over an appropriate time. Their eventual value is likely to be near zero without human intervention.

Then a broad measure can be deduced. The difference between current value and depreciated future value is equivalent to the value of people.

But this approach, like all the other attempts to account for the value of people, is fraught with difficulties and qualifications. In the end human asset accounting smacks of counting how many angels fit onto the head of a pin. It is more productive to assume that every enterprise has only one living substance – its people – and move on to consider how to obtain the best possible contribution from all of them. How to think about doing this is covered in other parts of this book.

Metrics are limiting

Henry Mintzberg, who has appeared before in this book, wrote a seminal work in 1994: *The Rise and Fall of Strategic Planning*. In a section headed 'The soft underbelly of hard data', he writes:

> The belief that strategic managers and their planning systems can be detached from the subject of their efforts is predicated on one fundamental assumption: that they can be informed in a formal way. To be more specific, detachment is possible only if the information they need can be provided conveniently.
>
> The messy world of random noise, gossip, inference, impression and fact must be thus reduced to firm data, hardened

and aggregated so that they can be supplied regularly and in digestible form … The message was as evident in the early years of the planning literature, which emphasised numerical forecasting and analyses of costs and benefits, as it is today, with the current interest in competitor analysis and shareholder value (which assumes measurable relations between strategies and stock prices).

For data to be 'hard' means that they can be documented unambiguously, which usually means that they have already been quantified. That way planners and managers can sit in their offices and be informed. No need to go out and meet the troops, or the customers, to find out how the products get bought or the wars get fought or what connects those strategies to that stock price; all that just wastes valuable time.

The deficiencies of 'hard' information are that:

- it is often limited in scope and lacking richness, and fails to encompass important non-economic and non-quantifiable factors;

- much is too aggregated for effective use in decision-making;

- much arrives too late to be of use for decision-making and taking action;

- a surprising amount is erroneous or misleading.

Soft information is supposed to be unreliable, subject to all kinds of biases. Hard information, in contrast, is supposed to be tangible and precise. It is, after all, transmitted and stored electronically. However, hard information can be and often is far worse than soft information. Quantitative measures are only surrogates for reality – whether a reject count in a factory as a surrogate for product quality, or a publication count in a university as a surrogate for research performance, or the number of operations completed as a measure of surgical performance.

Not just economic but socio-economic

All enterprises are socio-economic entities in that they live in complex environments and bring together a wide range of human and financial resources to create (mostly) something of use to the world around them. In this regard, they take energy from their environments and in turn give something back.

In one sense, all enterprises are akin to machines that use inputs – money, materials, services and peoples' skills – and process them to create outputs which are of value to customers/clients. The outputs are of two kinds:

- tangible and immediate, measured by success in meeting customer needs and the financial deficit or surplus thus created;

- intangible, such as reputation, impact on the environment or communities and contribution to knowledge.

Like machines, enterprises can be assessed by the efficiency by which they use resources and process them to produce outputs and outcomes. However, this has many limitations: in particular it does not recognise that enterprises can 'feed' off their outputs to grow, learn and improve.

If you view enterprises simply as economic systems, they have the virtue of being capable of creating:

- value for customers and clients through providing them with products and services that are worth more to them than their cost – they maintain this value through innovation and continuous improvement;

- value for suppliers of capital by generating returns from sales that exceed the cost of the capital after allowing for essential expenditure and investment – if they create positive value, they can reinvest part of this to improve and grow;

Figure 1 ■ Creating a sustainable enterprise

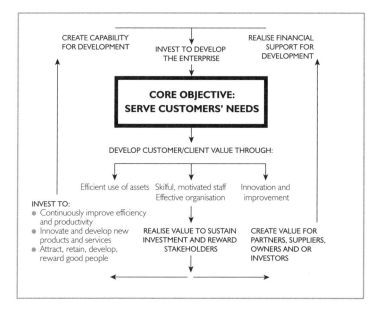

sustainable value through the quality and continuous development of their staff – this includes maintaining an environment in which staff can learn and also gain from the trust and social capital generated by their commitment to their colleagues and the purposes of the enterprise;

value through making a positive contribution to the community and creating valuable knowledge, receiving community support in return.

All these elements can be used to create the wherewithal for the enterprise to improve and grow.

These value-creating activities can be represented in the form of a virtuous cycle which enables an enterprise to create and use financial surpluses to reward suppliers of money and invest in people, innovation and product/service improvement on a continuing basis (see Figure 1). Of course, if it fails to create sufficient value, the virtuous cycle can become a spiral of decline.

Figure 2 ■ Socio-economic factors affecting organisational achievement

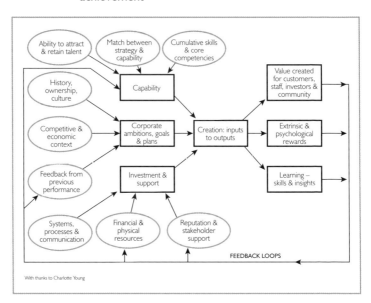

With thanks to Charlotte Young

However, the purely 'economic' view of enterprises is mainly financial in its focus and thus fails to place a value on such factors as culture and learning.

If you view enterprises as socio-economic systems, you take into account all the factors affecting achievement and sustainability. These factors are internal and external, financial and human, tangible and intangible. Figure 2 identifies key inputs and outputs to a range of stakeholders, and shows how learning and stored experience can make important contributions. At its heart is the organisation that converts inputs into valuable outputs. Lastly, it demonstrates that enterprises give to and receive energy from their external environments, and shows how feedback loops are crucial in maintaining the vital energy of enterprises.

The socio-economic model of enterprises

This model contains most of the factors that will affect an enterprise's performance and demonstrates that all enterprises take and receive from their surrounding environments.

Inputs

All the factors that determine the long-term effectiveness of the enterprise, including:

- financial and material support from suppliers and investors;

- the plans and ambitions of the enterprise, determined by appraisal of the environment, culture and history;

- the design and appropriateness of the organisation and the ability to attract, develop and deploy talent.

Creation: converting inputs to outputs

The means by which the organisation creates value by converting inputs to outputs. Every enterprise has internal processes that produce something of value for its customers/clients, investors, staff and the surrounding community.

Outputs

Enterprises can create:

- something of value to customers, investors/funders and the community around them (some destroy value, but generally not intentionally);

- learning and enhanced insights from experience;

- rewards for their members in the form of money, motivation and meaning.

Feedback loops

Most sustainable enterprises are like living organisms. They interact with their environments, giving to and taking from the world around them. Dynamic enterprises receive from their environments through the mechanism of feedback loops, which include: learning from experience; building a reputation with possible future employees and new customers; continuing support from the community, existing customers and investors; and enhanced motivation from the rewards and sense of meaning they create for employees. In this way virtuous relationships are created between inputs, outputs and the enhanced capabilities that sustain the future of the enterprise.

Why this model is important

John Kay commented in his book *Obliquity* that most worthwhile results can be achieved only by oblique means. He asserted that this is particularly true with regard to profit. His main point is that focusing directly on money and profit does not create superior financial performance – that comes from other, deeper sources. Profit is a by-product of getting a range of other things right. Obsessing about profit is likely to generate less profit than focusing on staff and customers.

Researchers have concluded that the reason for this apparent paradox is that the more successful companies concentrate primarily on factors that are not immediately concerned with producing profit or financial returns, such as employee skills and motivation, customer value and deep understanding of their business and its environment.

This model identifies most of the important determinants of sustainable achievement, and places financial value creation in its proper place alongside other equally important factors. But there is one area that is not properly recognised: customers, competitors and markets.

Customers, competitors and markets

All enterprises need to have a sharp focus on the customers they aim to satisfy, on the direct and indirect sources of competition for those customers, on the threats that could come from the competitive environment, and on maintaining or improving competitiveness and the quality of customer offerings.

Commercial, not-for-profit and public-service enterprises face these issues to some degree, but the nature of the threats to their existence may be very different. For not-for-profit enterprises, reputation and appeal to funders and givers are particularly important; for public-service enterprises, the major issues could be justifying the value of their services to society, and the different attitudes to public services of political parties; for private, for-profit enterprises, the competitive environment and the activities of direct and indirect competitors are of particular importance.

Competitive strategy

Any business strategy should have markets, customers, competitors, opportunities and threats at its centre. Large groups will probably operate in several industries, and the process of compiling strategies will have to be devolved. This creates difficulties for a holding group, which risks becoming a sort of investor/banker with limited understanding of its businesses. In the case of publicly quoted enterprises, the risk is compounded when group headquarters become investors, interacting or competing with another layer of investors in the financial markets. Dilbert would regard this role as 'of little use, and bound to fail'. Some may disagree, but they should think carefully about whether the added value derived from corporate activities exceeds the cost.[2]

Some elements of a market strategy

■ **Industry definition.** An industry is a group of organisations supplying products or services which are similar or close substitutes for each other. Enterprises should understand the dynamics of their industries and changes that have occurred or might occur.

- **The forces of competition, opportunities and threats.** These will include competitor activity and plans and the threats arising from substitute products.

- **Understanding markets and customer needs.** Segmenting customer groups in the market in terms of their needs and sensitivity to price and susceptibility to fashion changes. Clarifying the sizes and growth/decline of segments. Creating a strategy for each segment to meet customer needs and compete successfully.

- **Key success factors.** The small number of strengths that are difficult for competitors to copy and will ensure superior performance.

- **Competitive strategy.** Being clear about the combination of advantages that impels customers to choose an enterprise's products or services, and the operational capacity to deliver the chosen strategy. A strategy may be well-conceived, but will fail if the organisation cannot deliver it to a high standard.

Assessing achievement sensibly

Despite the comments about the inadequacies of 'hard' data, it is still necessary to generate numbers about trends, events and comparative performances. Such information matters, not so much because it tells the 'truth', but because it can act as a trigger for further investigation. There is no substitute for going and looking or talking to those who are in touch with the real world. Dilbert is absolutely right – anything that is more than one remove from the real world of frontline staff and customers or suppliers is subject to distortions.

Managers usually work by using all their senses in running a business and noticing and dealing with potential problems. In the event of something not being well the process might be as follows:

- Signal received that all is not well in a part of the enterprise. This could be a snatch of conversation, the emergence of dissonant information through the management information system, or simply an intuition that all is not as it should be.

- Seek data that will reinforce or refute the feeling of unease. Assemble a 'picture' that might contain feelings about the people involved (capabilities, trustworthiness, commitment), the context (market data, trends and pressures from the competitive environment) and the hard facts (financial trends, key performance indicators).

- Go and find out directly. Visit and talk to a range of people in various positions. Meet customers or clients if possible. Discuss matters with local managers and staff. Try to find out why as well as what. Get to underlying causes of problems.

- Conclude. Use experience, intuition and feel, and hard data to reach a conclusion about whether intervention is needed and if so, how it should be managed.

- Decide on a course of action. Involve others as necessary.

Sensible investors also rely on their intuition as well as hard analysis. Paul Hewitt, formerly deputy CEO of the Co-operative Group and now a partner at Lyceum Partners, a private equity group, described his approach to assessing the potential of prospective investments as follows:

- Take a careful look at the financial statements. Strip out distortions caused by accounting policies and other effects to get full visibility of the underlying metrics of the business – cash flow, costs, costs of capital and borrowings.

The aim is to get right to the base of the business to understand whether it is making money.

■ Then, if the figures look encouraging, put the financial information to one side and focus on what the enterprise is really good at. This can only be done by talking to key people at whatever levels are significant. This phase relies on intuition and the application of experience and judgement. I want to know if there is something special about this enterprise and the people in it that has and will create something distinctive and sustainable. This means I must know something about technologies and the competitive arena and how the market is likely to develop.

■ Then, I make an assessment of the people involved at the core of the business and whether I believe they have special skills and how committed they are.

■ After all this, I make a considered judgement on whether the potential of the business is sufficient to be worth investing in. Obviously, financial skills play their part, but observation and intuition are more important. I never want to invest in a business where I cannot understand the key drivers of success, whether these be technology or unique business formulae.

The fallacy of smooth, continuous growth

High-achieving enterprises will often enjoy periods of high growth, but this may not be their most important characteristic. The foundations of high achievement are primarily the quality of products or services and the ways in which enterprises relate to customers. Equally important is their strength and flexibility and the quality and commitment of management and other staff. All these factors will be subject to change over time.

Anything that damages these core strengths will inevitably damage the long-term prospects of the enterprise. In reality, the growth patterns of high achievers will be variable. There will be times when consolidation is needed to build the strength of the organisation; and there will be times when investments for the future will slow the growth of profit. Commercial opportunities and threats may also affect growth.

It is possible for an enterprise not to grow yet remain an extremely high achiever, efficiently supplying excellent products or services and providing satisfaction and development for employees. Growth is a stimulating condition for retaining good staff, but there are other ways of doing this; intrinsic and monetary rewards, comradeship, innovation, new technologies and new experiences are also strong motivators.

The continuous growth imperative that obsesses so many senior management teams is often driven by pressures from financial investors. These pressures can be extremely destructive, forcing managers to take huge risks, and often stem from the pursuit of mergers and acquisitions as a way of keeping growth going. A moment's thought will show that this kind of strategy is dangerous, especially if one believes that performance comes from the virtuous merging of the interests of staff and customers. Managers of high-performing enterprises are usually cautious about actions that may damage the fundamental strengths of their organisations, preferring organic growth and small, incremental acquisitions of enterprises in similar markets as their routes to growth.

Sensible observers and long-term investors will recognise that successful enterprises go through many different phases of growth and consolidation, giving rise to many different levels of financial performance. Equally, top managers will need to tailor their objectives and strategies to the dynamics of their own organisations and the markets they serve.

Obliquity reiterated

Enterprises cannot be satisfactorily valued through financial lenses, as they are human communities that live in complex environments. Metrics may give a limited snapshot of financial performance at a point in time, but they are flawed as measures of what may happen in the future or, even more important, of the roots of progress or decline. As for how future success may be secured, that needs a totally different frame of understanding and attention to essentials such as customers and staff – the served and the servers, in other words.

5. The contribution of the social sciences

The social sciences, put simply, are the study of human behaviour. Here, however, the simplicity ends. The social sciences have necessarily become fragmented into many disciplines. Psychology is rooted in the behaviour of individuals, singly and as members of groups. Sociology is the study of people in groups and communities. Social anthropology is the study of cultures and people organised in distinctive groups such as tribes and nations. I would include the study of history as a social science, as history is (or should be) the study of human events and behaviour over time. And economics should not be left off the list. It ought to be the study of humans and their behaviour related to production, consumption, money and work, and the impact of their economic behaviours on the wider society. Somewhere along the line something has happened, and economics has been captured by mathematical modelling and political dogma as well as invaded by quasi-science from other disciplines such as genetics.

The social sciences are powerful lenses through which to understand business and enterprise – a fact that is hugely underappreciated. The modern world has become transfixed by finance as the lingua franca of business. This trend has been described as 'financialisation'. In their book *Financialization and Strategy*,[1] Julie Froud and her colleagues describe how the fundamental nature of corporate strategy has been changed from a primary concern with customers and competitors to an obsession with the financial markets. They argue strongly for a rebalancing of the ways in which enterprises are appraised and managed. A more balanced approach would encompass finance, but particularly the social sciences. This is because most of the causal factors in business and public services are rooted in customers, organisations and their people. Financial measures alone are inadequate because:

- money is essential to running most enterprises, but it is inert – it can only be obtained, used and multiplied by people;

- most financial measures and statements are synthetic representations of something else – the something else being the products of people in organisations and customers in markets;

- financial statements may indicate that something is good, bad or indifferent at a point in time, but they are almost useless in describing why this is the case – and even more so in indicating what needs to be done and how. These need different dimensions of understanding and reasoning.

Business depends on people working together in organisations, some of which are highly complex. Organisations interact with their environments, especially their customers, through their staff. As consumers, people are motivated by a wide range of impulses, needs and wants. These are analysed exhaustively by social scientists working for advertisers and politicians.

Figure 3 ■ Organisations and the wider environment

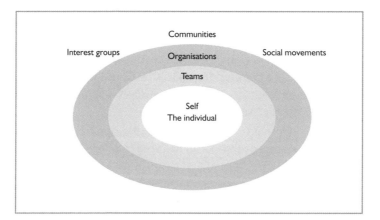

Communities

Interest groups
Organisations
Social movements

Teams

Self
The individual

The way organisations work[2]

People act individually, in small groups and in large crowds. How they act and react, how they can be motivated, how they are affected by history and different experiences can be best understood through social science lenses. An understanding of particular individuals and groups of people can be a powerful predictor of how events might unfold, as may be seen by the failure of economists and financial types to predict the recent banking crisis. The social sciences can therefore be useful in understanding how enterprises perform, but unlike finance, can be powerful predictors of future performance.

Figure 3 illustrates a model with individuals at the core. Then it widens out to consider people's behaviour when acting in teams and small groups. Wider still, the social sciences can give powerful insights into organisations, and then into the behaviour of people in communities and large groups.

People as individuals

Relevant fields: clinical, occupational and developmental psychology

This is the domain of psychology. The study of people and their behaviour is relatively new, starting in the nineteenth century and blossoming through the twentieth. The work of psychologists such as Freud and Jung has illuminated the previously hidden worlds of motivation and inner drives and anxieties. The professions of clinical psychology and psychiatry and the newer science of neurology (brain development) have given great insights into the relationships between physical and mental health and the impact of environmental factors on thinking and behaviour.

So psychology, if skilfully deployed, can be of huge benefit in describing and predicting the behaviours of people at work and can much improve thinking and decisions about the suitability of individuals for different roles and in different contexts. Hence it is not only valuable for selecting and matching people to situational demands, but also for helping individuals to adapt to new contexts and to think about their futures. Because of its importance, Chapter 6 describes how to work with psychologists.

People in small groups

Relevant fields: social psychology, group dynamics and such constructs as transactional analysis

The performance of even simple tasks often requires people to collaborate with others. This can be in temporary task or project teams, but often in more permanent working groups, called teams, boards or committees. Such groups can be minefields of conflict, misunderstanding and inefficiency, but if they are well-constructed and prepared, they are the only way of melding a range of necessary skills to produce the most complex and wonderful artefacts.

The functioning of teams has been the subject of much study and many books,[3] and much training material has been produced to help with 'team building'. An understanding of how different individuals respond in small group contexts, why conflict and ineffectiveness can affect particular groups and how to enable teams to develop effective working relationships is an essential part of effective organisations.

Organisations

Relevant fields: psychology, group dynamics, transactional analysis, social anthropology and sociology

Organisations are among the most complex creations of mankind. It is a truism that they are the vehicles which 'carry' all enterprises of any scale. Without the organised, co-ordinated and aligned efforts of many people with a range of skills and specialisations, virtually nothing would be done in the worlds of science, religion, business and social or public enterprise.

Yet many people's understanding even of their own organisations is inadequate to explain what is going on or to predict likely outcomes. For example, many senior managers are unaware of the relationships between the formal structure and hierarchy and the informal, hidden networks that help or impede getting things done. They too often act in ways that ignore the real but often invisible skeins of relationships, habits, assumptions and values that form the substance of most organisations, and they erroneously believe that every person's motivation and perceptions are the same as their own.

It is impossible to hold the complexity of any organisation in one's hand, but there is much useful research and guidance into how organisations work, and in particular how they can adapt and change.

Communities

Relevant fields: sociology and anthropology, relating to beliefs, roles, relationships and institutions in societies and how these contribute to well-being

Communities can take many forms. Towns and cities are communities of a kind, as are movements, sects, religions and political parties. Industries bound by common interests and values can also form communities. The investment banking industry is certainly a community in that it is bound by common interests, has a strong internal set of values, and has intense global communications between its parts. Individual organisations with long histories and strong shared values may be distinct communities.

Gillian Tett, a *Financial Times* journalist and an anthropologist by training, pointed out in her book *Fool's Gold*[4] that anthropology is far more useful in understanding the behaviour of investment banks than economics and financial modelling.

Understanding organisations

Organisations come in a vast range of sizes and shapes. Some are extremely old, like the Catholic Church. Some have risen and fallen, like the Hanseatic League and the Roman and British Empires. The oldest known company is Nisiyama Onsen Keiunkan (705), a Japanese hotel. Other examples are the UK's Royal Mint (886), Pontificia Fonderia Marinelli (1000), an Italian bell foundry, and Lowenbrau (1383), a German brewery.

Since the rise in power of the investment markets in the twentieth century, the life spans of quoted companies have dropped dramatically. Some put this down to 'creative destruction', one of the more outlandish ideas of free marketers. Organisations can be difficult to understand, particularly because most of their substance is invisible and cannot be measured or counted. The more ephemeral features are some of the most important. We cannot make sensible statements about an organisation's strengths and weaknesses without understanding its history and culture, the unwritten psychological contracts that govern what people will give to the organisation and the skills and competencies embedded in individuals, groups and functions. More tangible aspects such as reporting relationships and formal hierarchy, buildings, machines and systems are more easily understood, but the relationships between these tangible factors and the invisibles remain, well, invisible.

This complexity is why external observers without social science skills resort to simplistic measures like cash flow projections and the assumed character of the boss. It is probably why the performance of many institutional investors falls below the commonly used stock-market index yardsticks and is often little better than using blindfolds and a pin.

Understanding organisations is crucial for:

■ making senior appointments, succession and developing future leaders;

■ diagnosing strengths and weaknesses;

■ understanding the causes of performance shortfalls;

■ predicting future performance;

■ managing change and improvement;

■ planning and executing mergers and acquisitions;

■ crafting learning strategies and employee development.

In order to understand organisations, interested observers need to have a reasonable understanding of:

■ individual and social psychology (understanding leaders and senior people and the operation of teams);

■ anthropology (the behaviours and relations of people in groups in communities) – I would go so far as to say that embarking on a big merger without an understanding of

anthropology is like jumping out of a plane without a
parachute;

■ systems thinking – organisations are in one sense human
machines, but that metaphor should not be taken too far;

■ sociology – the study of large groups and populations;

■ the use of metaphors.

Two of the best contemporary thinkers about organisations
are Henry Mintzberg and Gareth Morgan.

Mintzberg described how the design and structure of
organisations should be contingent on the nature of the tasks
they had to perform. He identified a range of organisation types:

■ simple – with direct relations between boss and workers;

■ machine-like – capable of reliably performing repetitive
tasks;

■ flexible (adhocracies) – for project and creative work.

He analyses the parts of an organisation and configures
these into five ideal forms that enable people to think about the
nature and design of their own organisations. The essence of
his thinking is described in his book *Structure in Fives: Designing
Effective Organisations.*[5]

Morgan used twelve metaphors to describe different facets of
organisations, wisely contending that they are highly complex
organisms (a metaphor) that cannot be understood by one
simple description. Here are some examples of his metaphors:

■ Organisations as instruments of dominance. Anybody
working in an organisation dominated by bullies will
understand this.

■ Organisations as machines. A commonly used metaphor
that rather limits understanding of the richness of
organisations.

▨ Organisations as cultures. All organisations will develop commonly understood habits that eventually solidify into a recognisable culture.

▨ Organisations as organisms. Organisations give energy to an environment and receive inputs that are transformed into outputs.

Morgan's book *Images of Organization*[6] is strongly recommended to those interested in improving their understanding of organisations. In *Imaginization*[7] he uses pictures and other media to describe different forms of organisation suited to different purposes. One of his metaphors in that book is to characterise corporate staff in two ways: one is as bringers of central control and bureaucracy; the other is as bumblebees, which can fly from one part of an organisation to another, bringing learning and useful information and gaining new insights themselves.

▨ Communities and society

The systematic study of societies and how they function became established in the nineteenth century. The primary disciplines are sociology and social anthropology. But it must be said that the advertising industry, which in some countries exercises massive influence on the consumption patterns of millions of people, was greatly influenced by the thinking and work of Sigmund Freud's nephew, Edward Bernays, so a knowledge of psychology is also essential in understanding behaviours in society.

Sociology and social anthropology use various methods of empirical investigation and critical analysis to develop a body of knowledge about human social activity. For many sociologists the goal is to conduct research which may be applied directly to social policy and welfare, while others focus primarily on refining the theoretical understanding of social processes. Subject matter ranges from the micro level of individual agency and interaction to the macro level of systems and the social structure. At the level of individual enterprises, what may be of most interest is the use of psychological methods to influence and (maybe) manipulate mass opinion, inside or outside the organisation.

As previously stated, anthropology can be extremely useful in understanding cultural differences among groups, tribes and organisations. Thus military expeditions employ (or ought to) anthropologists to discern strategic cultural footholds; marketing people use anthropology to determine propitious placement of advertising; and humanitarian agencies depend on anthropological insights as a means of fighting poverty.

Important factors deriving from social science

Motivation at work

Motivation has been defined as the psychological process that gives:

- a purpose and direction to behaviour;

- a predisposition to behave in a purposive manner to achieve specific, unmet needs;

- an internal drive to satisfy an unsatisfied need;

- the will to achieve.

For the purpose of this book, motivation is defined operationally as the inner force that leads individuals to accomplish personal and organisational goals.

Fred Herzberg, an American psychologist, was influential in drawing attention to different factors affecting work satisfaction and motivation. According to his motivation-hygiene theory, also known as the two factor theory (1959) of job satisfaction, people are influenced by two sets of factors:

- Motivator
  - achievement
  - recognition
  - work itself
  - responsibility

Figure 4 ■ Ways of creating meaning

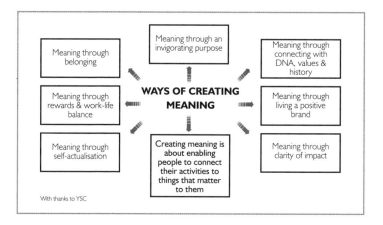

- promotion
- growth.

■ Hygiene
  - pay and benefits
  - company policy and administration
  - status
  - job security
  - working conditions
  - personal life.

Herzberg's most important point was that hygiene factors were not effective motivators, but they could be significant causes of dissatisfaction. The practical significance was that organisations should provide satisfactory hygiene factors and then concentrate on the motivators.

Meaning as a motivator

Gurnek Bains, chief executive of YSC, a consulting firm with expertise in psychology, and his colleagues put the fruits of their experience into a book entitled *Meaning Inc*. The thesis of their work is that once basics such as fair rewards have been dealt with, creating meaning through work can act as an important motivator. Meaning, to Bains, is 'enabling people to connect their work activities to things that matter to them'.

Figure 4 illustrates some of the things that YSC believes to be important. These include creating a sense of worthwhile purpose, attractive values and culture, and a 'brand' with a positive image; enabling people to find self-fulfilment through work; and creating a sense of belonging and fair rewards for effort and results.

Perception

There is no such thing in human relationships as objective reality. People will react differently to stimuli and events. Thus a decision or act that is seen to be based on simple rationality by one person or group of people can be interpreted very differently by others. Charlotte Young, a sociologist, describes how perception works:

> You become consciously aware of environmental stimuli and you begin to analyse and interpret the perceived 'objects' or events in order to give them meaning and context.
>
> How you analyse what you perceive will be greatly influenced by many factors including your past experiences, feelings, imagination, values, memories, beliefs and your cultural setting.
>
> Because the content and degree of these influences will be different for everyone, the same object or event can be perceived very differently by different people. This is why perception is not reality.

These observations are of critical importance to both society and organisations. Perception is at the root of many phenomena:

■ Conflict between different groups of people and between individuals. What may seem to be axiomatic to some will be anathema to others. For example, the statement 'It is axiomatic that shareholders own companies and may dispose of them as they wish' will seem obvious to many investors, but others may see it as denying the importance of the many people who create value in enterprises. To them, it represents a narrow legalistic definition of a situation that is archaic and unjust.

■ Conflict between leaders and others. Leaders may see themselves as having legitimate power because of their formal position, but this may be resisted or rejected as illegitimate by many in the organisation because they are considered to be uncaring or incompetent.

■ Confusion and disorder. People may perceive an important event or opportunity in different ways and act accordingly. This may be at the root of many military disasters.

■ Groupthink. If a tight-knit group of people have developed a common perception of the world, they may become cut off from others in their organisation, thus isolating themselves from important organisational information or, even more dangerous, from the markets it serves. This is almost certainly what happened to the senior management group at Marks & Spencer, a British retailer, before its slump in performance in the late 1990s.

Because people may attribute events and their causes differently, all managers must be aware that their perceptions are not objective 'truth'. They need to be clear about their values and beliefs and sensitive to the fact that many others inside and outside their organisations may see the world differently.

■ Understanding the human side of mergers and acquisitions

Top managers are often ambitious individuals with well-developed egos. For many of them, there is considerable appeal in leading a growing business, and often the easiest way to do this is by making acquisitions. CEOs of big companies have a limited average tenure (5–6 years) so the pressure is on to make a mark as quickly as possible. They are spurred on by the general belief in the financial markets and media that 'deals' are exciting, so reputations can be much enhanced by ambitious transactions. Investment bankers thrive on big deals – and the bonuses for a successful transaction can be huge. So, the climate around big business is febrile and bankers actively circulate 'ideas' for potential acquisitions. A friend once described introducing an ambitious CEO to an investment banker as akin to introducing a 16-year-old son to the madam of a brothel.

Before a merger there is frequently a kind of hunting ritual. The 'hunters', usually top managers, supported and egged on by investment banking advisers, plan the 'campaign'. The bankers stand to gain massively, earning a percentage of the gross value of the deal – not on whether it creates value. They become cheerleaders for the deal. The campaign, often conducted from bankers' premises in 'war rooms', involves valuation of the quarry, and planning and executing a PR and media campaign to persuade investors on both sides that great value will be created by the merger, usually through 'synergy' benefits. Synergy has become a euphemism for radical cost savings, although some lip service is often paid to the 1 + 1 = 3 benefits as well.

All this may appear to be quite rational, but it seldom is. Soon egos become inflamed, the quarry often campaigns hard against the deal, and the whole process becomes a kind of war game (defending managers also retreat to 'war rooms' with advisers in attendance to plan their campaigns). Sometimes the contestants become so involved in the fight that any semblance of rationality disappears and valuations become inflated, making it harder or sometimes impossible to realise value from the deal.

This is what happens before the merger. Now let's take a look at what happens afterwards.

It should not take too much imagination to guess what typically goes on inside two organisations that merge. No matter how good the planning by integration teams, there will still be a huge amount of disruption, usually for reasons that are basic, even primitive.

There will be competitiveness and defensiveness, there will be tribal behaviour, and there will be a sense of winners and losers.

There will be uncertainty among staff on both sides. People will spend an unusual amount of time on their own concerns. The two organisations will have different ways of doing the same things and there will be contradictory views about which ways are best. Systems, procedures and habits of behaviour will be different and people will not know what is expected of them. There will almost certainly be a lack of trust, so many people will be trying to second guess what others are saying. Nobody will take risks or embark on unnecessary initiatives.

There will often be a need for the 'losers' to mourn what they have lost and to come to terms with the fact that things will be different in the future. To cap it all, many people are likely to be losing their jobs, or facing job changes, with the inevitable disruption that this causes.

Frequently, in the rush to make quick 'synergistic' cost savings, people with valuable skills and knowledge will be laid off, and some of the company's future lifeblood of talented young people will leave because they see no opportunities for promotion.

Even the threat of takeover can cause disruption and stasis.

A director of a large company whose top management were willing participants in merger discussions reported that when the merger intention became known to the staff at large, 'everything just stopped'. Then the merger was reported to the competition authorities, which spent 15 months in a protracted investigation. 'The whole organisation froze for that period. Nothing was done beyond simply keeping the business ticking over. We lost a lot of ground to our competitors.'

This basic human and emotional stuff, usually invisible to the distant financially oriented folk who make and support the deals, is the main reason the majority of mergers and acquisitions fail to reach pre-deal forecasts.

It is estimated that 60% or more of larger mergers fail to create value, and those that do make money for the investors in the acquired enterprise, not the acquirer. Acquisitions that create value are often small ones of similar or complementary enterprises. One company made the managers who merged the acquisitions responsible for managing the whole process, and rewarded them for the value created after three and five years. This shows an understanding of the behavioural aspects of mergers seldom demonstrated by those who do big deals.

6. Business psychology

The scope of psychological study is large. It ranges from consideration of the human personality to what unites the human race and what differentiates individuals. It considers psychological illnesses and the physical factors that may influence pathological conditions. Psychologists can assess human intellect and how people develop and use their brains. The study of individuals crosses into the study of groups and communities, the bridging mechanism often being the investigation of people's social and relational habits and skills.

Psychologists come in many forms. It is important to assess whether particular individuals and techniques are going to be useful and valid. When choosing a psychologist, check for membership of relevant professional bodies and previous experience at the right levels. Do not use psychological tools or questionnaires without becoming qualified or without the support of professionals qualified to use them.

A good psychologist should be able to:

■ provide a far better understanding of people's drives and motivations, their thinking processes, relationships, working habits and preferences than a non-psychologist could, and apply this understanding to a complex working environment and its demands;

- make a large contribution to the assessment of individuals for appointments or promotion (and be proved right in most cases);

- coach and counsel in the case of problems at whatever level;

- assess people's potential for development and changes of direction;

- advise people on their developmental needs and how to meet them;

- assess the membership and likely interactions of people in teams or working groups;

- profile the abilities and values present in larger groups of individuals, for example senior managers as a cadre.

As well as individual psychology, such disciplines as social psychology, the study of human interactions in groups, can be of great value. Techniques such as transactional analysis from the work of Eric Berne,[1] FIRO-B (Fundamental Interpersonal Relations Orientation–Behaviour) by Will Schutz,[2] and Meredith Belbin's Team Roles Inventory are useful in helping teams to review their performance with the help of a facilitator. Some team inventories, such as the Team Effectiveness Survey by Francis and Young,[3] can also be helpful.

All these techniques can be useful in:

- constructing effective teams;

- diagnosing and rectifying problems in teams;

- understanding interpersonal issues in working groups;

- helping individuals to understand how to make effective contributions in teams or working groups;

- facilitating team development.

How enterprises can use psychology

In an organisational setting, psychology can provide a potent set of tools that can be used to enhance achievement.

Testing and biographical interviewing

There are two main approaches that psychologists use to assess people. The first is primarily test-based, using a variety of validated tests to measure aspects of personality, preferences and intellect. The second comes from clinical psychology, originally the study of disorders, and is equally effective for assessing the whole person and their relationships with the world around them. In business, it is based primarily on in-depth interviews by a psychologist, supplemented by a limited number of pen-and-paper tests.

Charles Mead, a director of YSC, has found the second method to be particularly acceptable to senior managers. He outlines the ways he seeks to help organisations and individual managers:

- First. The main limiting factor on the performance of any enterprise is the quality of its people. At the root of all enterprises in any sector are money and people, and it is people that make, use and attract the money in the first place, so having a rich understanding of the profiles of people in terms of their attributes and potential has to be a very potent tool. We can audit the quality and likely performances of individuals in a systematic way.

- Second. We can help managers to understand how to manage change and improvement and develop realistic expectations of the degree and speed of change an organisation can tolerate. An appreciation of the profiles of key individuals can inform thinking about what kinds of strategies will work and which will not, given the make-up of the people. Psychologists can help to predict how individuals and populations may respond and behave under a wide variety of pressures.

■ Third. We can help people to develop their potential and to perform well. Or rather we can help managers to understand how to support, guide and coach individuals. Psychologists can assist directly by coaching and mentoring people through enhancing their self-insight and understanding what kinds of jobs and organisational settings are likely to suit them best.

In his view, simply providing raw reports on people is of little practical value. A psychologist must work with an internal counterpart who understands the context of a particular enterprise and who, with the psychologist's support, can form judgements about people. If this internal person has a deep understanding of the strategies being followed by the enterprise and can provide insights into the implications of those strategies, then we are looking at a potentially very productive partnership. Not all senior managers are good at understanding the strategic context and its implications for people and organisations. But some chief executives and HR directors are – and a good HR director is an ideal person to work with, provided he or she is trusted by the top managers and involved in strategy.

Expanding on the contributory role psychology can play in business, Mead identifies four aspects: selection; developing potential and enhancing performance; supporting team development; psychology and the wider organisation.

Selection: a jointly managed process

Most important from the beginning, Mead says, I believe strongly in the fact that I have a responsibility to the individual and the client, and that we must try hard to give individuals value from the assessment process. In the case of YSC, this means giving them full feedback about the picture we have built of them. Having got this straight:

■ The first and crucial step is getting to understand the context in which individuals will be working. I broadly use the McKinsey 7-S model to inform my thinking. This entails thinking about shared values that distinguish the organisation's culture, the strategic direction and what demands that will place on people, and the prevailing style of the organisation: for example, is it collegial or individualistic, supportive or hostile? The model encompasses staff, which I read to mean what abilities and attributes will lead to success or otherwise in that organisation. Then there is the structure of the organisation to consider: is it informal or formal, is power centralised or devolved and are there many boundaries between functions and activities? Last and related to structure are systems: how formal are reporting, planning, performance management and people development activities and what impacts are they likely to have on approved behaviour? I guess that I now only use 7-S in an informal way, but it was helpful in my early days in practice.

■ Having gone through this kind of thought process, I like to generate an understanding of the pressures and opportunities that will demand change – how fast and how extensive – because that is likely to have a marked effect on the kinds of people who will be successful.

■ Then, because we are considering the selection of people for jobs, I want to understand the job context: how much freedom a job holder has to shape what is done, the nature of boss and subordinates, and the influences on the job of the surrounding organisational context.

This process can only really be successful if done in partnership with a knowledgeable insider.

The next steps are concerned with collecting and organising data about individuals. At this juncture, different psychologists will use different approaches. Put simply, occupational psychologists will lead with batteries of tests that define different aspects of individuals' personalities, drives and intellect, and then use experience and intuition to supplement the systematically generated data. YSC leads with biographical interviews that aim to unearth the patterns of influence that have shaped the person and their responses to the environment around them. This process I would describe as being akin to taking bearings on a person, and using the insights so derived to build a picture of the individual. We then supplement this information with data generated by inventories and tests, looking at intellectual horsepower and style, interactions with others, self-insight and learning styles.

There is evidence that senior people prefer the less structured approach, and that most appreciate the opportunity to tell their stories in their own way.

At this stage, I feed back my emerging picture of the individual so that he or she has an opportunity to challenge or confirm my early judgements. This is a crucial step in engaging with the individual and enriching my profile of them.

Then I write a report on the individual. This is quite structured; the structure is a discipline to help make the analysis stringent. The report covers the following dimensions.

Intellect

Intellect as measured by tests, with a focus on particular strengths and weaknesses – for example, numeracy and verbal skills – and as compared with populations of people in similar roles. Then, how they think and learn, the degree to which they are interested in new ideas and learning and flexibility of intellectual style, and whether they are broad thinking or more narrowly convergent.

Emotional make-up, values and motivations

How they deal with the world – the balance between emotions and feelings and thinking, and rationality in how they reach decisions and react to events. How they handle risk and whether they are consistent or unstable in difficult situations. What they like and dislike in a working environment and the ways in which their emotions may affect the manner in which they interact with others. Whether they are fundamentally open or prefer to be cautious in disclosing their values and views.

Key motivations: what 'turns them on' and energises them. What they find unacceptable in the behaviour of others. Whether they are fundamentally supportive or critical of others, and whether they prefer individualistic or collaborative styles.

Interpersonal factors

How they are likely to relate to others in a variety of different situations. Their skills in reading other people and in persuading or influencing them. How they will react to opposition or conflictual encounters. Their preferences for particular kinds of relationships: how they manage themselves in one-to-one, small group and larger set-piece situations. Whether they incline towards openness in their relationships or prefer to keep their powder dry and let others make the running.

Political astuteness: the ability to behave appropriately depending on the interpersonal dynamics of the situation.

Insight into self and others

How well they understand themselves and recognise their own strengths and limitations. Whether they can make sound judgements about the contexts that will suit their personality and skills. How well they are able to read others and understand what drives them, and whether they are able to use these insights for the benefit of the organisation. The extent to which they are able to reflect upon and learn from their experiences. Whether they are intellectually open and curious or conservative.

Work and management style

How they like to manage others – supporting and giving space to subordinates or preferring to closely control their work. Judgement and flexibility in handling different people in a contingent manner.

How they handle themselves in different contexts, how they respond to pressure; whether they can remain in control of themselves and their work in stressful situations. How they respond to being managed. What forms of managerial behaviour they prefer.

Self-discipline and the ability to remain clear about priorities. How they respond to ambiguity or complexity in the work environment.

Strengths and weaknesses for a particular job

What they will bring to the job; what impact the job will have on them. The kind of contributions they will make in the job. Factors to be aware of if they are in the job, including how to manage them. Longer-term potential and ability to grow over time. The fit between the job and their ambitions.

Making judgements and decisions

This is the point when we meld structured analytical data and intuition in order to consider the 'fit' between the individual and the role. This is when the client manager and the psychologist need to work together, the psychologist to bring a rich understanding of the individual, and the client manager to describe the content, demands and pressures of the job and the wider organisational context. It is also important that each of them understands the other's role in the process. It is useful if the client has a working knowledge of the basic concepts and methods of psychology and the psychologist has an understanding of organisational life.

Judgement questions

- What distinguishes this person from others?

- What are their particular strengths and weaknesses relative to other candidates?

- Is it likely that this person, in this context, will be ineffective, moderately effective or very effective?

- What are this person's strengths and potential vulnerabilities?

- What support are they going to need to fulfil their potential contributions and be successful in the job?

- How best might they be introduced into the organisation?

- What drives this person's expectations and will the job and enterprise be able to fulfil them?

- How long might the person wish to do the job? In which directions might their future development lie?

Should we hire/appoint to the job?

It cannot be emphasised enough that the process leading to a judgement requires rigorous analysis and skill on the part of both manager and psychologist.

Developing potential and enhancing performance

If psychologists have been helpful in selecting people, managers often ask them to help identify and assess talent. The assessment process may be similar, but the questions to be addressed can be rather different. When making judgements about potential, at least three questions are likely to be asked:

- What kind of potential do they possess? What kind of role might they successfully occupy in the future?

- How quickly might they develop? What forms of learning and experience would suit them best?

■ Who will share responsibility for helping them to think about their own development and to have realistic expectations?

In this situation, the partnership between an inside agent and the psychologist will be particularly important, especially if the psychologist is to work directly with individuals in a mentoring role.

When the issue is improving individual performance, the base data gathered by the psychologist may be the same, but the questions to be addressed will focus on the reasons individuals are not making the contribution they are capable of in a particular job and organisational context. Psychologists and managers can work together to understand what might be done with individuals to help resolve problems and enhance awareness of what shape the desired level of performance might take.

A second, increasingly common situation is one in which an enterprise is undergoing significant change driven by internal or external factors and the issues are concerned with predicting how individuals might respond to change, and what can be done to help them.

In both these situations, there must be a clear understanding between manager, individual and psychologist, and care must be taken that the psychologist does not become unwittingly involved in manipulating or damaging individuals. There have been examples of psychology being used to assess people, some of whom were then fired without being aware why. This kind of behaviour should be avoided at all costs. There are some agencies that purport to be able to match people to jobs by using computerised tests. This is not good practice and can indeed be misleading and damaging.

Supporting team development

Teams and working groups may encounter many difficulties that will undermine their effectiveness. Psychologically, two of the most important are a lack of diversity among team members, giving rise to potentially bad decisions not being challenged, and a tendency towards groupthink, whereby team members suppress their individuality and any opposition to the supposed cause. Such teams can preside over disasters great and small.

Psychology can help to support the development of effective teams by enabling members to understand and value their own contributions and those of others to the team's work.

In addition to the batteries of tests used by occupational psychologists, which can be helpful if all members have been assessed, there are several psychologically sound inventories that can be used specifically for team development. A commonly used one is the Myers-Briggs inventory,[4] derived from the ideas of Carl Jung; another is FIRO-B, which looks at the ways in which individuals interact with others.

Psychology and the wider organisation

The psychologists interviewed for this book freely admitted that one of the greatest challenges they faced was connecting their insights into people as individuals to an understanding of the wider organisation and its effectiveness. When experienced psychologists assess large groups of individuals at different levels in organisations, they can look for similar characteristics that may be shared by groups. For example, Malcolm Hatfield, an occupational psychologist, discovered that a large group of middle managers in one organisation tended to behave in a domineering way with subordinates and in a rebellious way with superiors. This was helpful in identifying the source of problems experienced by new top managers who were trying to bring behavioural change through the organisation. In the end, it was concluded that extensive changes were needed in middle management.

Some psychologists assess cadres of management, looking for significant characteristics and abilities that may distinguish the group, as well as uniformity or variety of characteristics and abilities among the group. The results can provide senior management with a valuable picture of the strengths and weaknesses of an organisation's managers when compared with a particular strategic direction or external challenges. Normally a degree of diversity of skills and competences is desirable. If an organisation is faced with the prospect of considerable change, it is crucial that senior management know how well managers will respond to the challenges.

7. Politics and power

The underlying purpose of this book is to help readers devise strategies that are intended to improve the performance of their enterprises. Almost inevitably this will mean the use of tactics aimed at influencing others to accept their diagnoses of what needs to be improved and what should be done about it. At this juncture readers will be engaging in a series of political acts, because one definition of politics is simply the process of persuading others who may be of a different mind to go along with a particular course of action. I recommend that readers should try to reduce the size of the shadowy side of their organisations in which covert deals are made, but it is impossible to remove organisational politics altogether. So the important thing is to use the shadowy side of organisational life to positively reinforce the more formal and open one, and work in both to ensure long-term success.

Most people working in an organisation will readily admit that they are surrounded by various forms of wheeling and dealing through which different people, groups, departments and alliances attempt to advance specific interests. However, this kind of activity is rarely discussed in public. The idea that organisations are supposed to be rational and their members seek common goals tends to discourage discussion or attribution of political motives. Politics, in short, is seen as a dirty word.

But in reality organisational politics is neither dirty nor clean *per se* – it just is. All enterprises with an organisation of any size are cockpits for politics, because different people will have different amounts and kinds of power, and differing views about what is good and bad and what ought to be done. The processes of resolving such differences are in themselves political – they may be violent, self-interested and negative or they may be well-intentioned and collaborative – but that is just a distinction between 'good' and 'bad' politics, not a denial that it exists.

Gerry Egan, in his book *Working the Shadow Side*, puts the case for confronting politics as a part of managing succinctly:[1]

> Given today's pace of business and institutional life, and given all the uncertainties of the business and economic environment, managers are increasingly being forced into the role of managing disorder and change.
>
> While the technology of such change is comparatively straightforward and easy, the politics of change can prove impossible. Thus, the best managers are always looking for ways to become more adept at dealing with the Shadow Side of the organisation – the unspoken, unacknowledged, behind-the-scenes stuff that stands in the way of getting things done efficiently, or even getting things done at all.
>
> In today's organisational and business climate, becoming skilled at behind-the-scenes management is not an amenity but a necessity. Failure to deal with the shadow side of change can lead to the failure of the enterprise itself.

So the reality of organisational life is that politics is inevitable, and high-achieving managers will use the process of influencing others to advance the cause of the enterprise, not simply their own power or interests.

The causes of politics

Organisations need to be ruled

Organisations of any size need the actions of many people to devise, design, make, sell and service their outputs, be they products or services. And such a social entity will need co-ordination, direction and priority setting to work. In other words, organisations need to be governed or 'ruled'.

In his book *Images of Organization*, Gareth Morgan puts it clearly:[2]

> Organisations, like governments, employ some system of 'rule' as a means of creating and maintaining order among their members. Political analysis can therefore make a valuable contribution to organisational analysis. The following are among the most common varieties of political rule found in organisations:
>
> - Autocracy: absolute government where power is held by an individual or small group and supported by control of critical resources, property or ownership rights, tradition, charisma, and other claims to personal privilege.
> - Bureaucracy: rule exercised through use of the written word, which provides the basis for rational-legal type of authority, or 'rule of law'.
> - Technocracy: rule exercised through the use of knowledge, expert power, and the ability to solve relevant problems.
> - Co-determination: the form of rule where opposing parties combine in the joint management of mutual interests, as in coalition government or corporatism, each party drawing on a specific power base.
> - Representative democracy: rule exercised through the election of officers mandated to act on behalf of the electorate, and who hold office for a specific time so long as they command the support of the electorate, as in

parliamentary government and forms of worker control and shareholder control in industry.

■ Direct democracy: the system where everybody has an equal right to rule and is involved in all decision-making, as in many communal organisations and kibbutzim. This political principle encourages self-organisation as a key mode of organising.

It is rare to find organisations that use just one of these different kinds of rule. More often mixed types are found in practice. For example, while some organisations are more autocratic, more bureaucratic, or more democratic than others, they often contain elements of the other systems as well.

Different interests

Different people, departments and parts of organisations may have different interests or be governed by different ideologies. In the old days, the personnel function was thought to be people oriented and 'soft' and the finance function analytical and concerned with the 'hard' side of business. This of course was rubbish, but didn't stop people being stereotyped as personnel or finance 'types' – and, of course, the personnel function attracted more women than men. Equally, design engineers and manufacturing people may be motivated by different things, as will sales people and accountants. In these matters perception is all, and failing to engage with others from different functions may breed damaging hostility and distrust.

What is in different people's perceived interests is frequently a cause of political manoeuvring between powerful people at the top of organisations, who use wile, guile and power to get their way. Out of such behaviour organisations can become riven by tribalism, or even open warfare between the followers of rival leaders.

Power

All organisations are cockpits for people to exercise power – from individual autocracy to direct rule by the many. But it is always important to bear in mind that power can be exercised for many purposes: some may be for the better interests of the organisation; some may be for the furtherance of personal interest; and some may be carefully cloaked in concealment – for example, pretending that self-interest is in the common good.

Politics and change

The management need for political stratagems is greatest when change is necessary because any significant changes are likely to affect the interests of different stakeholders in different ways. Seldom will a major change, however it is driven, engage the interests of all internal and external stakeholders in the same manner. Some may be in favour of the change, some may be strongly opposed, and some may be uncertain and willing to be swayed either way, depending on the strength of the arguments that they hear.

Different political strategies for different circumstances

Those who have to lead a change process need to be clear about what they are facing and then pretty smart when it comes to choosing the right tactics. Figure 5 may be of help in thinking about appropriate political strategies. There are two major dimensions to be considered when deciding on a strategy:

- the likely depth and extent of opposition;
- the amount of time available.

There are four main positions, each of which is likely to demand different, often completely different strategies:

- **Flight or fight.** If time is short and opposition is likely to be strong and extensive, leaders are faced with a stark choice.

Figure 5 ■ The dimensions of a strategy

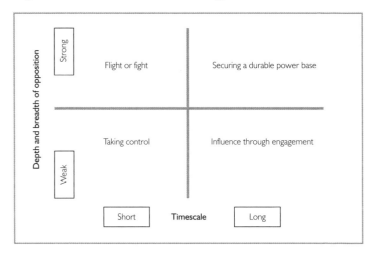

They can decide that the chances of success are too low in the time available and sensibly opt to seek their fortunes elsewhere, or they can decide to make a real fight of it. To stand a chance, a leader must start with a power base, and the first act should be to consolidate it, for example by finding like-minded influential people. For those who do not have such advantages, or are in more junior positions, the choices are stark – keep their heads down and hope to play a long game, or go elsewhere. If leaders decide to take on the opposition and play to win, they must be prepared to go to considerable lengths and deploy the full range of political tactics, including some that might appear to be underhand or brutal. Playing hardball politics is not a long-term strategy. If leaders pursue such tactics for too long, the organisation can become a poisonous place in which good people are damaged and the more unpleasant ones thrive. Such organisations never succeed for long. But leaders who decide to engage in battle must be prepared to go all the way to win. Withdrawal or hesitation before victory is a sure-fire losing game.

■ **Taking control.** When time is short, but opposition is likely to be sporadic or in small pockets, leaders must still be prepared to act forcibly to remove or convert opponents. This must be done, or opponents may make a tactical retreat in order to fight another day. So leaders who want to establish a firm base and avoid guerrilla warfare will be best advised to act firmly and quickly to neutralise opposition.

■ **Securing and extending a power base.** When timescales are more relaxed, but opposition is still likely to be strong, leaders can afford to plan their campaigns to establish power and influence with care. In this case, the aim is to secure a sound power base and then make it robust by all means available. There will be a much greater need for guile and subtlety, as such stratagems will almost certainly require the winning of hearts and minds of many people, and this cannot be done for long by brute force.

■ **Maintaining influence through engagement.** Even when opposition has been eliminated and the organisation is aligned with the leaders' priorities, there is no room to back off and disengage from the organisation. Leaders must maintain their influence and knowledge of what is happening through constant and close engagement with many people at many levels throughout the organisation. The established and savvy leader will use personal contact to 'read' the mood of the organisation, pick up important information and get messages across to a wide audience.

Actions leaders can take

Below are some ideas on the actions that leaders can take in the four scenarios depicted in Figure 5. Of course the four positions exemplified are seldom experienced as simply in real life, but making the distinctions clear helps in understanding that different situations need different responses. Also, my stance is that politics are best minimised.

Flight or fight

What to do when resistance is likely to be strong and widespread, and time is short. Power-use should be personal and formal stemming from an organisational position. Power is often exercised by an individual or a small in-group.

Anyone who is not in a formal position of power or is relatively junior has two only choices: find another organisation where they can make a positive contribution; or keep a relatively low profile, play a long game and start to look for allies. Managers who have a formal position of power should not rest on their laurels, for they are likely to be in a weaker position than their status may indicate. Assuming that opposition is likely to be deep and strong, here are some things that a change-minded leader can do:

- Find some allies, and quickly. In extremis, these may have to be previously known and trusted colleagues recruited from elsewhere.

- Make a 'political map', charting who are the key power possessors and speculating what their interests might be. Include an assessment of the strength of their following and potential weaknesses in their positions.

- Trawl discreetly for internal allies. Work to 'recruit' insiders to the cause, but be careful not to expose them to political danger; neutered allies are of little use.

- Declare a state of crisis. Develop a compelling narrative about the state of affairs and the dire consequences of failing to act. Use as many authoritative sources as possible to back up the narrative.

- Reinforce the crisis message by using short-term transactional methods to reduce the immediate problems. In a real crisis, the use of business disposals in conjunction with a process of replacing key people has sometimes resulted in a successful turnaround.

- Identify the 'commanding heights' of the organisation – those positions with the greatest leverage and power. Try to manoeuvre supporters into such positions or roles close to them.

- Watch the actions of opposing power-possessors like a hawk. It is important to maintain contact with opponents and enemies; deceit and dissimulation may be needed to keep the lines open.

- Use the planning and performance management systems to support the narrative and establish targets that will take the enterprise in the right direction. A good ploy is to introduce the planning process in an atmosphere of great urgency, using phrases like 'crisis planning', and then present guidelines that spell out the need for great change and improvement.

- Institute strong short-term inducements and rewards for actions and results that fit the narrative. In one company, six-monthly bonuses were introduced for specific actions and results.

- Get control of the recruitment and appointment system. This is a potent lever for making sure that the 'right' sorts of people get appointed to the key jobs.

- Get rid of key opponents by whatever means possible.

- Put about 'stories' that reinforce the narratives. These can be positive or negative – but it is essential to have a reasonable stock of believable and positive good-news stories.

- Move as rapidly as possible from this mode of operation towards a longer-term and more engaged position – managing crisis and brutal politics can be effective only for a short time.

Taking control

What to do when time horizons are short and resistance is less strong or widespread. Power-use should be more engaged but stemming from an extending in-group.

The situation may be similar to the first one, but it will differ in the sense that opposition is less formidable or more fragmented. But it is important for the leadership to get a firm grip on the reins of power and act quickly to remove opposition. Then a more extensive programme of engagement can be started to spread the message and extend the change-oriented ginger group as rapidly as possible. Here are some useful moves:

- Take rapid action to convert or remove dissidents, making sure that everyone knows why they have gone.

- Go for extensive engagement to make a personal impact on as many people as possible and to spread the word about priorities, opportunities and the consequences of failure to act to resolve problems.

- Develop a clear change narrative and use every possible means of spreading it. Use the narrative to highlight the benefits of unity and the strength of concerted action.

- Act to populate the commanding heights of the organisation with people of like mind.

- Use the planning and performance management systems to ensure that there is alignment of plans and that performance and progress are rigorously monitored. Key projects should be set up with frequent progress reviews.

Securing a durable power base

There is no crisis, so opposition is unlikely to be formidable; it is more likely that the wider organisation needs to be persuaded that the desired direction is compellingly attractive. Power-use should be more relaxed, stemming from engagement with a widening network of people and eventually spanning the whole organisation.

This situation, like flight or fight, requires that opposition be removed or converted, but as resistance will be weaker, the task is less onerous. Nevertheless, leaders should not relax. After all, the long run consists of a series of short runs. Change-minded managers may have more time to persuade and convert as many people as possible, but should still be ruthless in removing those who could act as powerful blockers of change. Here are some ideas for this position:

- Continue the actions started in the crisis, especially those concerned with removing resistors and gaining control of the commanding heights, but introduce the concept of developing critical masses of people who are for the new regime and what it stands for.

- Develop a strong narrative about the necessity for change, but this time make it compellingly attractive, emphasising the huge benefits to be gained from seizing the opportunities that change will bring.

- Place as many disciples in the commanding heights of the organisation as possible. Also start to seed the organisation with high-grade people of potential. Institute a process for identifying such people, and make sure that they are drawn from all over the organisation. Control their development programmes in order to create networks of people who are imbued with enthusiasm for the changing strategy and the values associated with it.

- Establish extensive contact with as many people as possible across the organisation. Ignore hierarchy and emphasise openness and the need for all to sing from the same hymn sheet. Use the contact to find out what is happening, listen to people's concerns and do something about legitimate ones. Use all opportunities to spread the message – be remorseless and repetitive.

- Introduce staff development programmes across the organisation and ensure that they are consistent in style and content with the key narratives and values.

- Extend control of recruitment and appointment to more junior levels to ensure that the right kinds of people continue to spread throughout the organisation.

- Control the media, ensuring that all messages are consistent.

- Modify the incentive and reward programmes to emphasise longer-term and less financially defined progress.

- Increasingly use planning and performance management systems to emphasise joint responsibility for success. Make planning a more widely participative exercise.

Influence through engagement

Serious opposition has been removed and timescales are relatively long. The overriding objectives are to maintain a sense of direction and cohesion and to reinforce key narratives about culture and priorities. Leaders should engage strongly and extensively with the wider organisation to listen and spread their messages.

This is the default position to be aimed for and will lead to less need for politicking. The aim should be to foster collaboration and extensive engagement leading to mutual agreement and openness. It is nevertheless important to keep supporters aligned. Here are some useful ideas:

- Constantly reinforce narratives about priorities, events, successes and challenges. Leaders must make a point of meeting people at all levels in the organisation to show interest, listen, and give them an opportunity to make their views about what is important clear.

- Emphasise intrinsic rewards and advancement on merit. Money should be regarded as a 'hygiene' factor, but staff

should be well paid by comparison with peers. Make
the working environment interesting through extensive
involvement and devolution of responsibility. Publicly
celebrate positive behaviours and successes.

- All forms of learning and induction should include a strong
  element aimed at supporting the enterprise's values, history
  and excellence.

- Basic training in understanding the business and what is
  meant by good performance should be commonly shared
  by staff at all levels, so that common information systems
  can be used for communications about performance and
  priorities.

- Training should encourage extensive networking among
  staff at all levels, so that mutual support and help can
  be generated. Staff should be encouraged to rotate
  jobs in order to create mutual understanding – for
  example, head-office staff could work at the front line in
  manufacturing, sales or customer service.

- Selection and development should be strongly managed
  to ensure that the people selected for advancement have
  the attributes, values and capabilities needed to take the
  enterprise forward.

- Differences of view and perspective should, as far as
  possible, be exposed and worked through. Differences
  should be reconciled and decision-making processes should
  allow for open discussion and debate, but it should be clear
  how final decisions are to be reached.

- Those who engage in covert politicking or who seek to
  hide their intentions and performance should be dealt
  with severely. As a director of one successful large company
  said: 'You do not get punished for falling short of targets,
  provided it is signalled early and we can all work on

rectifying the problems. But those who try to hide problems or act out of self-interest won't last long here.'

■ Ploys and plays

Many commonly used political games are unpleasant and dysfunctional, being used to gain advantages over others for reasons that are not to do with furthering the aims of the enterprise. But some can be used for positive purposes to get things done in ways that might not be so effective if pursued through formal channels. The following list is by no means comprehensive:

■ Putting people down in front of others. In effect, causing others to lose face by pointing out mistakes, peccadilloes or weaknesses. 'Given his/her lack of experience, we can't expect them to understand what we (the rest of us) are talking about' might be a typical example, usually spoken in a faux-kindly tone.

■ Forming a coalition ahead of the event. This ploy can be used for positive or negative purposes, but the underlying intent is to outmanoeuvre opponents by facing them with a fait accompli when the matter at hand comes up for discussion.

■ Another version of the same kind of ploy is to refer a matter up to a higher authority, having 'fixed' the more senior person ahead of the event.

■ Ambushing the opposition. Ambushes are usually carried out in public meetings. The aim is to use the occasion to surprise the opposition with new facts or support from higher authorities.

■ Acting faux-naive. This can be a subtle ploy, especially if played by juniors on more senior people. For example, a subordinate was instructed to find and appoint a candidate that suits the senior. 'I am sorry to be so stupid,' said the subordinate, 'but could you give me your wisdom on why they had to have attended school Y and university X?' The subordinate kept on gently asking for the wisdom of the senior who became inarticulate while trying to avoid saying that the candidate should be of a certain social class.

- Flattery can be a potent weapon, especially with certain kinds of male. The aim is to cause powerful people to become so pleased with themselves that they forget to check on the fine print of a proposal or let apparently small matters slide through their scrutiny.

- Causing confrontations and rows on minor issues, losing them and then sliding the real issue forward for agreement a little later.

- Knowing what really motivates potential opponents and modifying an agenda to give them a good slice of what they want. This can be a positive ploy, using empathy to deduce what others want and pushing through the main agenda while giving them enough to satisfy them.

- Political mapping is a useful technique that works along the same lines. It involves 'charting' the major stakeholders who will be affected by a change and postulating what their positions will be and how to bring them on side.

- Maintaining hidden agendas. The proponent hides their real intent behind a cloak of pretence and concealment.

- Divide and rule. Usually the intent is to maintain control by dividing potential opposition. An example is to deliberately and publicly set up two candidates for advancement. One company nearly always had two contenders for the top job engaged in fierce guerrilla struggles while the incumbent kept control by simply stoking the flames.

Healthy habits

My intent is not to promote damaging political games, but to help readers recognise unhelpful political games when they are played and design win-win strategies.

The best counter to negative and covert games is to expose them, emphasise openness and state matters as they really are. However, even this healthy habit needs to be practised with care and a degree of discretion, as some powerful political players react badly when their games are spoiled.

When Gerry Egan ran a workshop for senior managers and started to reveal the secrets of the shadow side, an Italian manager vigorously denounced the exercise as worthless and damaging. Eventually, he stormed out of the session. One of his colleagues commented that he didn't like having his operating methods exposed in public.

Mediation and reconciliation can be used to great effect to defuse potentially damaging conflicts. Mediators normally work separately with each side to explore their positions and attempt to edge them closer together. This can only be done by a trusted third party and may take a long time. Mediators need to guard against becoming permanent go-betweens. Although this may be the only way of getting things done, it is usually unstable and can be exhausting for the mediator.

I should emphasise that any process of getting agreement and alignment of effort in organisations will inevitably be political. Positive players will use the political process to influence and move decisions and events in a positive direction to further the enterprise's objectives. Negative ones will use politics to advance their own cause. It is crucial to recognise the differences.

8. Synthesis

Synthesis is the combining of the constituent elements of separate material or abstract entities into a single or unified entity (as opposed to analysis, the separating of any material or abstract entity into its constituent elements).

The modern world of enterprise has become specialised, with finance and law being dominant in Anglo-Saxon economies, which are strongly influenced by investment banks and the financial markets. The tendency towards specialisation has been encouraged by many business schools, which still 'teach' management in specialist segments, such as finance, strategy, marketing, organisational behaviour and human resources. The use of cases to illustrate more integrated approaches to management does not go far enough in demonstrating how the best managers really work. Cases encourage analysis, rather than synthesis and the use of experience, intuition and rationality.

'Hard' facts and numbers from a management information system may help in indicating that something is going awry in an enterprise, but they give little help in determining why things are going wrong, who may be causing the problems, what to do about problems and how to take remedial action. This will require information derived from direct observation, meeting people, intuition and experience as well as the (often inaccurate) products of a financial reporting system.

Effective leaders must be able to work in many dimensions, rapidly assimilating masses of formal data and sifting out what is inaccurate or downright unhelpful. They must be able to use their experience without being trapped by their past. They must know when to listen, when to advise and when to instruct. They must be able to draw on others' skill and expertise. Above all, they must know when to go and look for themselves and not get trapped in their corporate ivory towers. They must recognise the limitations of their experience and knowledge and learn how to build teams that can cope with the complexity of the business as a whole.

The combined attributes of a balanced team should enable them to understand the enterprise and its environment as a whole. To do this they must be able to synthesise a mass of information coming in different formats: some numerical, some verbal, some verifiable and some speculative.

What competences are needed to craft and lead a complex enterprise in a changing world?[1]

Several dimensions need to be integrated in thought, planning and action:

- **Economic factors for competitive success.** Understanding the economic dynamics of industries, markets and businesses, and the factors that will make a competitor successful. Assessing the opportunities and threats facing an enterprise.

- **Choosing and using appropriate financial metrics for a particular enterprise.** Different enterprises need different measures. For example, a capital-intensive business will require an appreciation of the efficient use of capital; a retail business will need to measure footfall and sales per square metre.

■ **Organisational design and troubleshooting.** Diagnosing and describing an organisation's strengths and weaknesses, identifying gaps in organisational capability and defining actions that will improve effectiveness. Describing and predicting the effects on business performance of organisational strengths and weaknesses – in ways that add value to others' contributions and positively complement the finance function's perspective – especially when a top team is considering an acquisition, for example.

■ **Mediation.** Mediating between powerful individuals with large egos and strong self-interests in order to find a common agenda and alignment for strategic action.

■ **Counselling and coaching.** Counselling and coaching managers and staff to help them understand and cope with the business and the personal challenges facing them.

■ **Understanding and managing change dynamics and levers.** Understanding the dynamics of change in large organisations and what leverage will be most effective. Knowing what to change and what to foster and support. Planning and monitoring complex change projects.

■ **Using learning strategies.** Using learning to formulate strategy, and to support change and the development of new organisational competencies.

■ **Connecting planning and information systems so that business and organisation strategies are integrated and progress can be monitored.** Designing processes that will routinely connect analysis of the strengths and weaknesses of an organisation, and key staff, with the evolving business goals and strategies. Developing systems that will provide information on improvement or degradation against the critical signs of business performance.

Last but not least, effective senior management teams will contain, or have access to, the requisite specialist and technical skills that pertain to their business.

What intellectual and personality factors characterise a good synthesiser in a leadership role?[2]

Individuals will:

- be broadly observant and notice links, connections and patterns formed by events and 'hard' and 'soft' information;

- form tentative hypotheses about problems, opportunities and actions required;

- seek additional information to confirm or refute their hypotheses through more hard data and through conversations with a wide spectrum of people within and outside the organisation;

- distinguish between issues that need immediate or short-term decisions and longer-term ones that need further exploration before action;

- carry a personal agenda in their heads and constantly discuss this with people at many levels to communicate what they think is important and gain further perspectives from others' experiences.

Constructive synthesis: an example

The subject is a large international company that was part of a larger group. The CEO of the parent group was anxious about the deteriorating financial performance of the business. He discussed his concerns with the business's CEO, and received assurances that improvement was under way. He also had many meetings with his staff, in particular the finance and HR directors. These two had different perspectives. The finance director could see only that the business was a drag on the group and the trends seemed to be getting worse. It would be best to dispose of the problem and sell the business. The HR director was equally worried, but had a strong feeling that the business was badly organised and led. It would be best to find out more before taking such a drastic step.

The CEO wanted to find out more about the industry and its prospects before acting. They hired an external consultant who, after carrying out a quick study, reported that the industry was healthy with good growth and margins for the leading players, but that the business in question was grossly underperforming in international markets, though its performance in some markets was good.

Group management concluded that the problems were internal – if other players could perform well, there was something wrong with leadership, marketing and organisation. It was imperative that they get a better perspective, and so over a period of months they and their staff visited many locations and talked to numerous people in the entertainment business as well as outsiders in touch with the industry. The CEO and HR director went out of their way to cultivate relationships with the business's CEO.

At the end of this process they reached the following conclusions:

- Divisional management were deliberately bending the finances. The corporate costs of the division were being farmed out to operating companies and the accounts falsified to give the impression of improvement.

- At the individual country and regional levels, there were some outstanding performers.

- Local managers were angry about and disillusioned by the behaviour and incompetence of international marketing and the arrogance of international headquarters.

- The division was being run as a kind of fiefdom for the benefit of the CEO and a small number of cronies.

- These problems would not get better under the existing leadership; there was a need to replace the CEO and several other key players.

- There were several talented regional managers who would blossom if the dead hand of the CEO and his cronies were removed.

Working together and with a business psychologist over a period of two years, the group CEO and HR director persuaded the business's CEO to step aside and accept a replacement.

A replacement CEO was found after an extensive search and careful psychological assessment. He had good credentials in companies that were leaders in international marketing. Several of the regional managers were promoted; the majority of divisional staff were replaced. The second key appointment of director of international marketing was made with the full agreement of the new CEO.

The divisional HR and finance managers were replaced. In addition to competence and ability to work with corporate colleagues, openness and integrity were key factors in their selection. The financial reporting systems were completely overhauled and matched with the planning system.

Over the next three years, the business's performance progressively improved. At the end of five years it was among industry leaders in terms of market shares, profits and growth.

Lessons

- Cross-functional collaboration by people who respect each others' competence is crucial.

- The numbers were important at the beginning, but as signals of other wider problems. They were also unreliable.

- There is no substitute for going and looking, and talking to people on the ground; you will never pin down the real causes of problems from a remote distance.

- The solutions were mainly organisational and people-related, but the reporting systems were also completely revamped.

- Many inputs and perspectives were used – marketing, financial, systems, organisational, individual performance and behaviour. The project would not have succeeded without them all.

Workbook

Planning and enacting an improvement programme

Introduction

T his book is intended to stimulate thought leading to action. Parts 1 and 2 describe what facilitates and impedes high achievement, the enduring values and practices contrasted with the fads, fancies and whims that offer false promise. Part 3 aims to help you convert ideas to action.

To make progress it is necessary to be realistic about the strengths and weaknesses of your organisation: what needs to be changed and what needs to be preserved. Self-insight should be combined with an understanding of organisational politics, in particular whether powerful influences are ready for, or can be influenced to accept, change. Then any change process needs to be contingent and appropriate. For example, fostering revolution when progressive innovation and adaptation are more appropriate is a recipe for disaster. The degree to which the wider organisation needs to be involved in initiating change – as opposed to accepting top-down direction – is also a crucial element in determining success or failure.

Last but not least, success depends on doing the right things as well as doing things right. There is a huge body of evidence and research into what works – what stimulates high achievement –

and what doesn't. Much of this evidence is ignored by pushers and promoters in the business education and consulting worlds, many of whom are more concerned with stimulating the market for their services by pretending to have discovered 'secrets' and new paradigms. Sensible leaders will take most of this material with a pinch of salt – and listen instead to the wisdom of those who have bothered to go to the coalface and observe what actually works.

The Workbook contains three sections:

- a questionnaire with some notes on understanding the dimensions that make successful enterprises;

- an analysis of strategies for managing change;

- suggestions for designing and implementing an improvement plan.

Before getting started: some things to think about

Don't make false starts

Creating expectations and then dashing them can cause disillusionment and alienation. Make sure that the conditions are right before starting on change programmes.

Secure a sound power base

If there is uncertain or insufficient support from those with the power to advance or undermine a change initiative, pause and check again. Make a realistic assessment of the commitment and interests of key individuals, institutions and interest groups, and continue to do this as change processes advance. Lone crusaders for improvement can be rapidly sidelined, so be sure to recruit support.

Assess the skills and resources needed

All change processes are complex to manage. It may be necessary to take people from their 'day jobs' to support aspects of change. Extra resources may need to be brought in to help. Be clear about what additional skills are needed, and in particular make sure that the responsibility for planning and action remains in-house. Use external consultants sparingly to coach and supplement insiders.

Use this book as a resource

Parts 1 and 2 can help in forming a rounded and integrated understanding of your enterprise. Inputs to thinking and action are likely to come from various sources and will be used in making diagnoses and deciding on courses of action.

Most people have preferred ways of thinking. Some are fixated with numbers and lists, regarding feelings and soft data as questionable. Such people often think convergently and are impatient to close down discussion and make quick decisions. Others rely on past experience and 'feel' and are concerned with broad pictures. Some think and act conservatively, even when radical action may be necessary. Others are hell-bent on making big decisions and big moves.

It is important to have a blend of approaches, but do not let the more extreme characters prevail. Equally important is having a blend of experience and knowledge. Good judgements and decisions require emotional maturity and flexibility of thought, as well as a sense of appropriateness. Most importantly, effective decision-makers must be able to synthesise many different forms of information by having an understanding of financial and non-financial metrics; using pattern-making and having the ability to imagine different possibilities; personal direct observation, relating authentically to many different people, weighing their inputs and making nuanced judgements from a plethora of inputs; using partial or imperfect information to make 'best-fit' judgements.

The questionnaire

The questionnaire and accompanying material are designed to help you analyse your enterprise's strengths and weaknesses and identify significant issues that may need to be addressed. This can be of use to the following:

■ Business students, who may find a sound non-financial business diagnostic to be refreshingly helpful.

■ Long-term investors, who may want to develop their repertoire of skills for understanding businesses, generate interesting questions about particular companies, and contemplate how they might find the information that will most reliably guide investment decisions.

■ Employees, who may wish to understand what is wrong with their employing organisations and agitate for change – or if this doesn't generate results find a better place to work.

The questionnaire is an enhancement of one originally developed by Don Young and Dave Francis, an experienced consultant and business writer. It is consistent with research carried out on the characteristics of durably successful companies by such writers as Jerry Porras and James Collins in *Built to Last*, Jay Lorsch and Gordon Donaldson in *Decision Making at the Top*, and many others. It is also generally in line with the results of a major study carried out by André de Waal (see Chapter 2).

Like any material of this kind, it provides a snapshot of the current situation, but is of course affected by the subjective views and knowledge of the users. It can be helpful in indicating where further investigation might be productive – and of course can reveal areas that are hidden from the users' gaze. One productive way of using it is to ask a number of people from the same organisation to complete it and then compare their results, highlighting similarities and differences for further discussion. The questionnaire is a way of shaping a programme of research and improvement. It will not reveal the 'truth', but rather the values and understanding of its users. It is therefore only one of a number of different perspectives provided by this book.

The questions are listed in groups under 14 headings, which are explained in some detail on the facing page to enhance users' understanding of what lies beneath the surface in sustainably high-achieving organisations. But there is a health warning: enterprises may score highly and still not be high achievers, for success also comes from intelligent leaders pursuing sensible strategies and staff who are up to the job, are concerned to contribute, and possess the requisite skills and competencies. This material will not reveal whether particular strategies can lead to success in particular contexts, or whether leaders and staff are up to the job, but it can stimulate thought about capabilities and the strategies in use.

Respondents are asked to answer each question with one of the following:

■ Mainly true of the organisation under consideration.

■ Mainly untrue of the organisation under consideration.

■ Unsure or don't know.

The questions

Responsiveness to the external environment

1. Management emphasises contact with the outside world.

2. Care is taken to understand what current and potential customers need and want.

3. Competitors are carefully studied. Strengths and weaknesses against competitors are systematically and honestly analysed.

4. Social, political and economic trends are understood and assessed as opportunities or threats.

5. Managers stay in touch with influential external bodies.

6. Employees at all levels are encouraged to look outside and bring ideas for improvement.

7. Planning processes encourage awareness of the market and competitive environments.

8. Frontline staff's opinions are regularly canvassed to assess competitor actions and customers' reactions.

The enterprise is open to external feedback and not in danger of being caught out by unexpected events or trends.

- High-achieving enterprises are constantly in touch with the external environment. They can monitor and read signals that may indicate a need to adapt what they do. Information from the front line is easily able to reach the top of the organisation and constant internal dialogue means that all staff are aware of imperatives for change.

- Strengths and weaknesses are honestly evaluated, employees are encouraged to look outside and bring ideas for improvement.

- Great care is taken to regularly canvass customers and frontline staff to assess the effectiveness of the customer offering and what may need improvement.

- Social, political, environmental and economic trends are constantly monitored and assessed as opportunities or threats.

- Weakness in this dimension can lead to complacency, blindness to changes in the economic and competitive environment, and a failure to adapt. Enterprises that have shown this characteristic have encountered serious crises or failed.

Developing and sustaining identity and culture

9. Top management recognises the importance of supporting a well-defined and distinctive corporate identity, which is more than words on paper.

10. Corporate personality and values are seen as essential sources of corporate strength.

11. Top managers act to demonstrate and articulate clear values that differentiate the organisation from other concerns in similar lines of business. These encompass factors such as 'the business we are in', 'what makes us successful', 'what we will always strive to do' and 'what we will never do'.

12. The values, principles and policies that define the fundamental character of the organisation are kept fresh through words and behaviour. They are open to periodic questioning to test their continuing relevance to changes in the environment.

13. Beliefs are well-defined about what fundamentally matters and what is superficial and can be easily altered.

14. The culture strongly supports action, informed by concern for long-term consequences.

15. Organisational leaders are visible and in personal contact, and have a strong positive impact on the internal audience.

16. Mutual respect is a clear hallmark of the relationships between top managers and other employees.

17. The organisation's name and visual symbolism are used internally as well as externally. Reports about the enterprise and its activities in the community and success in the market are widely communicated.

18. Selection and promotion emphasise people whose values and competencies are consistent with those of the organisation.

19. Those whose behaviour offends the values of the organisation are dealt with, to discourage others from doing the same.

20. Newcomers are carefully inducted and informed about the organisation's history and values.

21. Employees are able to articulate their organisation's key goals, standards and beliefs. People do not adopt cynical attitudes towards corporate 'propaganda'.

22. Common purpose is deliberately generated through personal contact, wide involvement in business planning processes and well-designed communications.

The enterprise has a distinctive personality that pervades everything it does and acts a source of motivation and meaning for staff.

■ Research shows that durably successful companies know who they are. They possess strong values and an enveloping personality and culture.

■ This pervades the organisation from top to bottom and strongly influences behaviour, both internally and towards customers.

■ The identity of the organisation is strongly represented by senior managers, who have an intimate knowledge of their organisations and consistently express its values by words and actions.

■ Corporate personality stems from knowing customer needs and serving them well, and from understanding what differentiates the company from its competitors. The products or services provided to customers are a rallying point for all and a source of pride.

■ Commitment to the enterprise and what it stands for is deliberately encouraged.

■ Newcomers are carefully inducted to their jobs and given strong guidance on what the enterprise stands for.

■ Those whose behaviour does not gel with the values of the organisation are informed and counselled, but if their behaviour persists, action is taken to discipline them.

■ Weakness in this dimension can lead to internal conflict, confusion about priorities and a lack of direction. Organisations that lack a strong identity can also fail to create a sense of meaning and employee commitment.

Planning and objectives

23. Long-term planning is designed to involve a wide range of people with relevant knowledge and understanding of all facets of the business.

24. Decision-taking is guided by a balanced concern for today's performance and the long-term future.

25. The organisation has effective processes for connecting broad statements of strategic intent to clear goals, measurable objectives and specific programmes of action. This means that employees are clear about their objectives and priorities, and how they connect to those of the wider organisation.

26. Employees in general know the performance targets for their work and are required to judge whether they can meet them. They understand how their performance will be evaluated.

27. Senior management ensure that planning and performance-monitoring systems link levels, functions and units, so that plans are integrated and all necessary contributions factored into action plans.

28. Planning encourages the consideration of options and contingencies so that the organisation is able to respond to changing circumstances.

Processes for planning and looking forward embrace all levels and communicate purpose, as well as being a source of learning.

■ There are effective processes for looking forward and setting goals, objectives and plans. Goals are consciously set to encourage continuous improvement and high achievement. Planning involves a wide spectrum of the organisation's membership and is the responsibility of those that will implement the plans. Units, functions, teams and individuals are clear about what they are trying to achieve and how it contributes to the success of the wider organisation.

■ Decision-taking is guided by a balanced concern for today's performance and longer-term viability.

■ Planning encourages the consideration of options and contingencies so that the organisation is able to be responsive to changes in circumstances.

■ Planning processes are reinforced by appropriate information and rigorous processes for reviewing performance; negative variances are rapidly identified and action is taken to bring improvement.

■ High performance is well-rewarded and underperformers are supported to help them improve. But, in the end, underperformance is not tolerated.

■ Weakness in this dimension can mean that plans are not enacted as a result of a lack of understanding and commitment from employees in general. It can also mean that strategies and plans are ill-conceived, lacking important information and insights from key parts of the organisation.

Control and performance management

29. The level of policies, procedures and rules is sufficient to guide employees but does not stifle initiative.

30. People understand what authorities they have and when to refer to others for authorisation. Wherever possible, authority is passed down the organisation to those immediately involved.

31. All levels of staff and management feed off a common database, so that action can be effectively co-ordinated.

32. Management information covers all aspects of performance (not just financial), is timely and accurate, identifies variances from plan rapidly and enables rapid action at the most appropriate levels.

33. Numerical information is balanced by feedback on on-the-ground realities.

34. Information processes generate information about problems and point to why they are occurring.

35. Resources can be quickly mobilised to deal with problems.

36. Top managers are closely in touch with the 'pulse' of the organisation, through formal and informal channels.

37. Group and individual achievement are clearly defined and monitored and clear feedback spells out areas for improvement.

The enterprise is capable of rapidly responding to performance variations and problems; its information systems enable the mobilisation of effort to address performance problems.

- Control policies, procedures and rules are sufficiently clear to guide decisions at all levels, but not oppressive so that they stifle initiative.

- People understand the extent of their authorities to decide and act. Wherever possible, decision-taking authority is devolved to the lowest level. There can be informal understandings between managers and subordinates so that capable staff are given the maximum latitude to act in the interests of the enterprise.

- Goal-setting is clear – people understand the criteria for judging their performance.

- There is a common base of data about performance that is accessible to all levels.

- Management information covers all aspects of performance. Numerical and formal information are balanced by understanding of the on-the-ground realities.

- Senior managers are in touch with the 'pulse' of the organisation through formal and informal channels.

- Information processes generate timely warnings about problems and point to the reasons for their occurrence.

- Resources and effort can be quickly mobilised to deal with problems.

- Weakness in this dimension can lead to a sloppy and inefficient use of resources, and failure to generate and use information about the 'vital signs' indicating underperformance. Overdependence on formal information and metrics can lead to a lack of realism about performance and problems. Effective organisations have sufficient control mechanisms to inform and respond, but do not stifle initiative.

Reward, sanctions and motivation

38. The reward systems are used as tools for supporting high standards.

39. Performance measurement, feedback and pay systems help motivate people to be highly committed to achieving the organisation's goals.

40. Reward is both psychological and financial. Incentive pay is not used as a substitute for positive feedback and celebration of a job well done.

41. High achievement attracts markedly superior rewards, shared by individuals and teams.

42. Low performance is systematically identified, with steps taken to deal with difficulties. Persistent non-performers are dealt with decisively.

43. Promotion and career progression go to people who have demonstrated superior merit.

44. Pay differentials between the top and the rest of the organisation are widely known and capable of internal justification.

45. People throughout the organisation feel that the reward system is clear, predictable and fair.

Rewards are clearly tied to performance and emphasise psychological as well as financial aspects. Financial rewards are transparent, widely understood and felt to be fair.

▩ High achievement attracts markedly superior rewards, shared by individuals and teams across the wider organisation.

▩ Rewards for performance are psychological as well as financial; people are generally motivated to do a good job without financial inducements. High performance is communicated and celebrated across the organisation. Low performance is systematically identified, the causes are investigated, and steps are taken to deal with difficulties.

▩ Persistent low performers are dealt with after being given support to improve.

▩ Promotion and career progression go to people who have demonstrated superior performance and merit.

▩ Pay differentials between top management and the rest of the staff are widely known and capable of rational justification.

▩ People throughout the organisation feel that the reward system is clear, predictable and fair.

▩ The commonest problem in Anglo-Saxon organisations is growing differentials between those at the top of the enterprise and the rest of staff, causing alienation and demotivation. Employees like to understand how they will be rewarded and sanctioned, and what performance and contributions may be rewarded. Underlying all this is the emotionally important aspect of 'felt fairness'. Failure to develop and enact clear and felt-fair reward practices will result in demotivation and a strong lack of commitment to taking initiatives that are helpful to the enterprise.

Organisation fit for purpose

46. The organisation is well designed to achieve the outputs required of it. It is designed to specialise in its particular business.

47. It is possible to identify clearly the unique contribution of each organisational layer from top to bottom.

48. The organisation operates through appropriate structures, systems and processes.

49. When circumstances change, the organisation can rapidly evolve to meet new demands.

50. The work of the component parts of the organisation is well co-ordinated. Tribalism and empire building are heavily discouraged.

51. Delegation and devolution of authority are encouraged and employees at all levels are encouraged to take initiatives and accept responsibility.

The organisation is designed to fit the business and is a source of strength, minimising fragmentation of effort and enabling staff to give of their best.

■ It is clearly understood that the quality and effectiveness of the organisation are the key to competitive success.

■ The organisation operates through appropriate structures with clear delegation of authorities.

■ There are effective co-ordinating mechanisms uniting specialist units and functions.

■ Integration of effort is achieved through effective standing teams and special project and problem-solving groups.

■ The organisation is shaped to the needs of the business and continuously adapted as circumstances change and new opportunities or threats emerge.

■ This usually means that change is progressive, continuous and actively involves the whole organisation. Sudden, convulsive, top-down change is avoided.

■ There is no universal 'right' form of organisation. The design, structuring and working of the organisation will be contingent on the type and context of business. For example, enterprises that depend on differing local markets may need a high level of devolution of authority; others may require strong central decision-making at a detailed level.

■ Organisations requiring high levels of creativity are likely to need informal, flexible, project-based management; whereas those in crisis may need strong personal direction. Failure to understand the need for flexibility and responsiveness will lead to underperformance and possible failure.

Appropriate skills and resources

52. There are effective information systems to enable management to know the capabilities the organisation possesses and realistically assess its capacity to perform in relation to the demands on it.

53. The strengths and weakness of people, systems and processes, key specialisms and productive facilities are rigorously reviewed against changing requirements.

54. Senior managers can compare current capabilities with their best guess of what will be required to achieve objectives. When gaps are identified, the stops are pulled out to develop missing capabilities.

55. People are carefully selected and stretched but also supported to reach superior performance levels. The aim is to have sufficient capability to maintain high standards and achieve stretching targets.

The organisation is well-resourced, with sufficient capacity to devote to future development and respond to unexpected opportunities or threats.

▓ Operations are well-resourced to keep them at the peak of effectiveness; investment in people, systems, equipment and productive facilities is sufficient to stay at the cutting edge.

▓ The strengths and weaknesses of people, systems, key specialisms and productive assets are rigorously reviewed against current and future needs.

▓ All resources – people, facilities, processes and practices – that have become obsolete or redundant are stringently shed.

▓ A spirit of enquiry, self-review and challenge of the status quo is encouraged.

▓ Failure to create the appropriate levels of resources to meet the needs of the moment and devote to future development can lead to inefficient sloppiness or under-resourcing of key activities, leading to long-term underperformance. It is important to keep the balance right and consciously plan and deploy adequate resources for present and future requirements.

Elimination of waste, redundant resources and outdated practices

56. The 'resources bank' of the organisation is rigorously evaluated in order to shed unnecessary costs and capabilities.

57. The costs of owning or hiring resources and capabilities are measured.

58. Causes of profligacy and waste at all levels are identified and removed.

59. Facilities, equipment, systems, habits and people that have outlived their usefulness are changed, redeployed or shed.

60. Policies and practices that no longer fit the contemporary context are eliminated or changed.

61. The organisation avoids doing things simply out of habit or tradition.

62. The ethic of caring for people or their sensibilities is not allowed to obstruct the strategic logic of maintaining just enough capability to meet present and planned needs.

There is constant review of the resources and practices needed to remain fresh and sharp. Anything that is not needed is eliminated and outdated policies or practices are dispensed with as new ones are introduced.

▓ Causes of duplication, profligacy and waste are identified and removed. All practices are examined as to whether they contribute to performance. Those that do not, including privileges and perks, are eliminated.

▓ The ethic of protecting people is not allowed to obstruct the need to maintain enough resources to meet current and planned needs.

▓ The costs and benefits of owning or hiring assets are constantly reviewed.

▓ Many organisations fail to review stringently policies, practices and resources needed for optimum performance. This can lead to gross inefficiency and the 'storage' of redundant practices and people, with serious long-term consequences.

Pride in the product, provision of meaning

63. The enterprise's products or services are a rallying point for employee identification.

64. Product quality, value, intrinsic worth and distinctiveness are such that employees can take pride in the product and therefore the organisation that produces it.

65. Senior management care about the product, not merely seeing it as a means to an end. They concern themselves with its value and quality, and respect the people who design, make and sell it.

66. Senior managers spend regular time at the customer and production front lines.

67. Employees in general know what the enterprise's end products are and get regular feedback about customer esteem. Efforts are made to expose as many people as possible to customers.

The worth of the enterprise's products is a source of pride for staff and can act as a rallying point for motivation and commitment. The experience of working for the enterprise gives meaning to employees' lives.

■ People at all levels believe that the organisation's mission to serve customers is worthwhile and a source of pride and commitment.

■ Senior managers manifestly demonstrate their commitment to the success and survival of the enterprise and evoke similar commitment in others. They clearly demonstrate commitment to the product, not seeing it merely as a means of making profit. They concern themselves with its value and quality, and show respect for the people who design, make and sell it.

■ The quality of their work and organisational membership give meaning to employees' lives – it is clear that people care about the organisation and its products.

■ There is increasing evidence that organisations where people have a sense of commitment and feel that their work has meaning operate efficiently without the need for excessive and costly control and inspection procedures. Organisations deficient in these dimensions can be costly, barren and ineffective places of work.

Care for people

68. Managers are concerned to make employees' work stimulating and satisfying

69. The behaviour of top management encourages employees to respect the organisation and devote care and attention to making it successful.

70. Co-operation and helpfulness are encouraged.

71. Employees feel that the leaders of the organisation are there by merit and have personal integrity.

72. People feel that top management is concerned about their well-being. The quality of employees' working lives is seriously considered by managers.

73. There is a sense of comradeship among the workforce that is reinforced by a degree of affection towards the organisation.

74. There is an explicit or implied 'contract' between the organisation and those who work for it, which recognises employees' needs for job interest and satisfaction as well as material reward.

75. Welfare and social activities that strengthen the organisation's sense of community are encouraged by top management.

76. Working facilities are designed to encourage human contact, without unnecessary divisions between different categories of employee.

77. Where decisions have to be made that have an adverse effect on employees, casualties are treated generously and with dignity.

The organisation, through the behaviour of its senior managers, demonstrates that the motivation and satisfaction of staff are its main priorities.

■ Co-operation and helpfulness are encouraged and there is a sense of comradeship among staff that is reinforced by affection towards the organisation.

■ People generally know their senior managers and feel that they are concerned about their well-being. There is an implicit contract between the organisation and those who work for it that recognises employees' needs for job interest and satisfaction as well as material rewards.

■ Working facilities are designed to encourage human interaction without unnecessary divisions between different categories of employee. Top management encourage welfare and social activities that strengthen the organisation's sense of community.

■ Where decisions have to be made that have an adverse impact on people's lives, casualties are treated generously and with dignity.

■ Organisations that are not felt to have a genuine regard for their people will fail to generate co-operation and commitment. They will also find it more difficult to enact hard decisions affecting people without creating resentment and alienation.

Concern for the community

78. Top management demonstrates a balanced concern for all key stakeholders. The interests of owners and shareholders, the wider community, customers and suppliers are all taken into account in top-level decision-taking.

79. The organisation behaves in an open and responsible manner in relation to key stakeholders and the public.

80. Employees are encouraged to make contributions to the local and wider society. The organisation makes efforts to support charitable, artistic and educational institutions.

81. Senior managers pay serious regard to the ethical conduct of the organisation.

82. All are aware of the enterprise's impact on the physical and community environment and efforts are made to reduce negative impacts.

83. On balance, the enterprise does more good than harm in the world.

Senior managers demonstrate that they do not let the needs of one stakeholder override the legitimate interests of others. They understand the importance of the enterprise being a good citizen and making a positive contribution to any community in which it is involved. This concern encompasses strict avoidance of causing environmental damage.

- The organisation behaves in an open and responsible manner in relation to key stakeholders and the public.

- Senior managers pay serious attention to the ethical conduct of the enterprise and encourage all employees to do likewise. The interests of owners and shareholders, employees, the wider public and customers are factored into top-level decision-making.

- Employees are encouraged to make contributions to the local and wider society. They are given time to make contributions to charitable, artistic and other worthwhile causes.

- On balance, the enterprise does more good than harm in the world.

- This dimension of corporate behaviour is slowly becoming more important. Organisations that fail to be, or pay lip service to being, good citizens will suffer from lack of employee and community trust, which can have negative economic consequences.

Governance and top-level direction

84. Those who violate ethical or legal standards are sanctioned – even if the enterprise would gain.

85. Senior managers work effectively together, with evident mutual respect, and are able to constructively resolve conflicts among themselves.

86. The board and/or top team are well-balanced, well-resourced and proactive. They see their primary role as being to promote and safeguard the long-term health of the enterprise.

87. Directors have the range of skills appropriate to the particular business and its circumstances. If necessary, additional specialised resources are bought in to supplement existing competences.

88. The enterprise uses independent external directors or advisers to bring fresh views and challenge on strategic matters.

89. External directors or advisers spend enough time on the enterprise's business to understand the operations and organisation from first-hand experience. They are not simply reliant on written and verbal reports or management's say-so. They are available to the whole top team and not just one member.

90. The process of the top team is open and robust. Debate can be intense without souring relationships excessively. Divergent views receive a good airing and are factored into decisions.

91. Where they exist, board subcommittees are well resourced and prepared to be pro-active – for example, the remuneration committee will initiate proposals for reward strategy, rather than wait for management's proposals.

92. The board as a whole, but in particular independent directors, are capable of robustly resisting external pressures if they believe that the best interests of the enterprise will be jeopardised.

Senior management pays serious attention to the legal and ethical standards underlying the enterprise's business practices. Governance issues are treated seriously at the top level, but are not allowed to override a primary concern for the long-term health of the enterprise.

■ The board or top team contains the range of skills required to understand and direct the enterprise. Where there is a formal board, independent directors are encouraged to bring an objective perspective to strategy formulation and ensure that all the enterprise's affairs are carried out with integrity. Independent directors spend sufficient time to gain in-depth and personal exposure to the enterprise's operations, so that they are not solely dependent on management or formal reports for their understanding.

■ The top team's processes and relationships allow open, frank debate where contrary opinions can be freely expressed. The team is cohesive and capable of strongly withstanding external pressures if they are not in the enterprise's long-term interests.

■ Those who violate the ethical or legal standards required are rigorously sanctioned, even if the enterprise benefited from their actions.

■ The organisational apex is important as the ultimate arbiter of strategic direction and standards. Too many boards or top teams are not sufficiently in touch with the wider organisation to be able to exercise effective leadership or co-ordination. Some of the greatest corporate disasters are the result of senior management action that lacked a sense of proportion or care for the wider organisation.

Bonding, trust and cohesion

93. Senior managers are clearly seen as an integral part of the organisational community.

94. Employees know senior managers as real people and trust them accordingly.

95. It is clear that their overriding obligations are to the success and long-term health of the enterprise.

96. Senior managers understand the business from first-hand experience and spend considerable time with customers and the front line of the organisation.

97. While senior managers take their obligations to external stakeholders, particularly investors, seriously, they do so recognising that that long-term value comes primarily from organisational excellence.

98. When the organisation is subject to adversity, it is clear that top management will share the burdens and pain equally with other categories of employee.

There is a bond between senior managers and the wider organisation, forged by personal exposure, common experience and a shared understanding of the enterprise's business.

■ Top managers are clearly seen as an integral part of the organisational community. They are widely known and trusted as real people. It is understood that they must pay attention to the interests of several stakeholders, but that their primary allegiance is to the long-term viability of the enterprise is never in doubt. In times of adversity, it is clear that the pain will be shared equally by top managers and other categories of employees.

■ Rewards are carefully designed to avoid excessive differentials and are capable of being explained and justified to internal and external audiences.

■ The era of 'shareholder value' and financial market-driven governance has not improved long-term corporate performance or durability. Senior managers that fail to understand the roots of high achievement and bond with their own organisations are likely eventually to end up destroying them.

Learning and development

99. Top management's time horizons stretch beyond the current generation.

100. The enterprise has a strong commitment to learning and all staff are encouraged to be curious and exploratory.

101. People at all levels are strongly encouraged to develop their talents.

102. Change is adaptive and continuous, so that it has become the norm.

103. Development practices emphasise tradition and progress equally.

104. Management development emphasises a spirit of enterprise, deep knowledge of the business and acute awareness of developments in the wider world.

105. Learning and education processes encompass all from entry level to the top.

106. The enterprise ensures that all employees have the same basic understanding of the business and can read and understand basic performance data.

107. It is impossible to reach top management in this enterprise without a balance of experience in several key functions.

108. The design of learning processes is based on combining learning with doing.

109. Good and bad experiences are openly reviewed by a wide spectrum of people as an opportunity for learning.

110. Most development programmes are managed internally. External contributors are carefully briefed to be relevant to the enterprise and its culture.

111. Career development processes are comprehensive and taken seriously by top management. The aim is always to develop succession for the top roles from within the organisation.

Learning is a major strategic element: planning, performance review and the success or failure of major projects are all used as sources of learning. Planning for and the preparation of succeeding generations of leaders are taken seriously. It is usual for top appointments to be made from within the organisation.

■ The enterprise has a strong commitment to learning and is curious and exploratory. Development practices emphasise tradition and progress equally. Learning and education processes encompass all from entry level to the top. All employees have the same basic understanding of the business and can read and understand basic performance data.

■ The design of learning processes is based on combining learning and doing. Most development programmes are managed internally; external contributors are carefully chosen and briefed to be relevant to the enterprise and its culture.

■ Career development processes are comprehensive and taken seriously by top management. The aim is always to develop succession for the top roles from within the organisation. It would be unusual for anybody to reach the top job without experience in several functions.

■ Market fundamentalists invented the concept of creative destruction. The idea was that assets should gravitate to those best equipped to manage them and enterprises that were inefficient would fail. This notion seems to ignore the fact that organisations and individuals can learn and thus adapt to the world around them. It is in only a tiny number of instances that organisations should inevitably fail.

■ Most enterprise failure is a result of a failure to learn and adapt. There is too little understanding of the practicalities of creating effective organisational learning.

Using the questionnaire

The questionnaire is intended to stimulate thought and discussion. It is best used by groups or teams to elicit a variety of perspectives – it would be surprising if every member of a group or team had exactly the same perspective. It will also reveal where respondents are unsure of the situation in their organisations. Senior managers are often not close enough to their organisations to know how people respond to the initiatives they generate and may be surprised by unexpected resistance or responses. This material may encourage them to go and check what is going on.

The questionnaire is not a scientifically precise instrument, but it is consistent with a large body of good research and evidence from many sources about what factors are most important in generating sustainable high achievement. A word of warning: no material of this sort can address some important questions that are fundamental to success – for example, the intelligence and personal qualities of leaders and the nature of the challenges facing the enterprise.

Scoring the responses

To generate discussion and understanding, there are three scoring possibilities:

- The statement is generally true. This would indicate an opinion that the dimension is a strength that should be preserved or enhanced.

- The statement is partially or mainly untrue. This would indicate a view that the dimension constitutes a probable weakness that needs to be addressed.

- The respondent is unsure of the situation or does not know whether the statement is true or untrue. This might indicate an important need to investigate and find out more.

Respondents should then apply a ranking of 1–3 to the dimensions that are rated as weaknesses. This will indicate whether these:

- will have a significant impact on performance and must be addressed;
- are significant, but not a priority;
- are relatively unimportant at this time.

The same procedure should be applied to the dimensions rated as strengths, indicating which are most important to enhance or preserve, and to 'don't know' or 'unsure' responses, indicating which issues are the most important to investigate further.

Using the results

There are several productive ways to use the material:

- For individual thought and reflection. It can help people at almost any level to think about the organisation and assess what works and what does not, and to consider what is most important and what might be done.

- As a means of generating discussion and exploration in groups, which could range from seminars to working teams. It can be particularly useful in mixed-status groups from the same organisation, as it will highlight similarities and differences of perspective. It is important that more senior people do not squash or take lightly others' opinions, as this will reinforce views that will probably not be openly expressed.

- As a means of preparing the ground for a more thorough examination of an organisation's strengths. Considering the questions can clarify thinking about what needs to be examined and what is most important for a particular enterprise. It can also be used for project teams about to embark on interviews.

Try not to be too precise in responding to questions and do not agonise over each detail. When the questionnaire is completed, it should be scored for each respondent:

■ Each negative response indicates an area of concern, which may need further consideration for action.

■ Each positive response indicates a potential strength, to be built upon.

■ Each don't know/unsure response may indicate an area for further investigation.

You should also note which sections score most and least strongly (less than 50 per cent positive could indicate a significant weakness). Also, individuals may feel that some questions are of more importance than others and should note these.

Suggestions for group discussions include the following:

■ Each individual should display their responses, and time should be given for consideration of the similarities and differences between them.

■ The group should consider the differences and why they have occurred.

■ Where there is consensus, indicating a need for improvement, the group should aim to rank issues in importance and decide what could be done to make improvements.

■ The group should decide what to do about issues where there is insufficient information to be clear.

Individuals can use a similar process, ranking issues and deciding which are the most important. It will then be useful to find ways of engaging others in discussion about the issues and what might be done about them.

The results can be of particular value when considered and discussed by a management team or groups of employees to explore views and identify strongly held concerns that may begin to form an agenda for action.

Strategies for managing change

The world surrounding most enterprises is constantly changing. Changes in consumer behaviour, fashions, technology, political priorities and competitor pressures mean that organisations that are not attuned to their environments will eventually atrophy and fail.

Other pressures for change will come from inside. Changes in leadership, power struggles, generational handovers, changes in employment law and employee expectations will generate pressures to adapt.

As change is a constant in the modern world, managers should be so attuned to coping with it that managing change is a default position for any competent leader. Yet there are numerous examples of failure to cope with change effectively. There are two main causes of failure:

- **Insulation and complacency.** Many enterprises have failed or stumbled into crisis because their managers and staff succumbed to complacency and resistance to signals that change was necessary. Marks & Spencer, a British retailer, is a good example. In the late 1990s, autocratic senior managers became isolated from their frontline

staff and customers, chasing the holy grail of profit to
such an extent that the very existence of a totemic brand
was threatened. Senior managers who become isolated
from their own organisations and customers have been a
common feature of British industry – think of motorcycles
and automotive manufacturing. (Luckily the Japanese came
to the rescue.) More recently, in the UK auto manufacturing
has been revived by Tata, an Indian company, which has
invested heavily in Land Rover/Jaguar; and in the US the
carmakers have been bailed out by government. The sight
of senior auto company managers arriving in Washington
by company jet to beg for money outraged the nation
and showed how far they had grown apart from the real
world. In the financial sector, Lloyd Blankfein, CEO of
Goldman Sachs, described himself as 'doing God's work',
while investment banks that have been bailed out by
government seem to believe they have a right to continue
much as before. European companies, which have boards
that contain representatives of the workforce and local
communities, have been much more open to external
reality and consequently there have been fewer examples of
disastrous decline.

■ **Impatience, short-termism and wild ambitions.**
Overambitious strategies based on flawed thinking have
destroyed large numbers of once-successful companies.
Think of AOL Time Warner, the creation of a wild vision
of synergy between enterprises that might have come from
different planets, doomed to disastrous failure. A common
thread is ambitious leaders who believe that there is a short
cut to success based on mergers and transactional strategies
that are popular with the financial markets. In recent years
an obsession with the financial markets and the media has
brought many companies to their knees.

It is crucial that leaders understand the dynamics of change and possess a wide range of often subtle skills that will enable them to carry their organisations with them.

Transformation: the rainbow illusion

Change is often misinterpreted as transformation. Transformations are often assumed to be the creations of inspired leaders who have a 'vision'. Transformation is therefore portrayed as a deliberate strategy of extensive change that will affect the character of an organisation and what it does. On the whole this is nonsense. Most transformations are achieved over long periods of time as a result of many adaptations, small steps forward and many experiments, some of which work and some of which fail. The nature of the transformation can only be understood over a long time and in retrospect.

Often experiments fail to achieve the expected results and are abandoned or used as learning experiences. The intention of sensible leaders in these cases is usually to make progress in small increments, not to change everything at once.

Attempting transformations in established organisations is hugely risky. The reasons are not difficult to imagine. Employees are asked to believe in a vision of a radically different future. They are expected to abandon beliefs, habits and practices with which they are familiar and follow the leadership into the unknown. There is likely to be scepticism, doubt and resistance. Different factions will form; established relationships will be broken or strained. Achieving such miracles is at the outer edges of possibility, but the risks of failure are high. Incremental change and adaptation are far more likely to succeed. I have searched my memory and asked many people to name an organisation of any substance that has successfully managed to transform itself – not one came to mind.

Examples of disastrous attempted transformations in established organisations are not difficult to find: Enron and Marconi, which both claimed to have developed visionary new business models, are two. The truth is that transformations usually happen in organisations without the kind of historical baggage that impedes change or in small enterprises dominated by inventive individuals.

A strategic change model

The model described here will help clarify thinking about what kind of change your organisation faces. There are four positions (two sets of two):

- Transformation and crisis management represent exceptional circumstances and need to be addressed as special cases. Neither is for the faint-hearted and both need exceptional treatment led by exceptional people.

- Continuous improvement and building are default positions. Both are rooted in an organisation's history, culture and core competencies, but they can be differentiated from each other by the enterprise's degree of long-term ambition for growth or new market penetration. For example, Japanese companies that grew outside their home markets in the twentieth century were extremely conservative about their core competencies, cultures and values, but ambitious to grow in international markets. James Collins and Jerry Porras described this approach well in *Built to Last* as the yin and yang philosophy of 'Preserve the Core – Stimulate Progress'.

Initially, you should consider how to manage two fundamental aspects of strategy: time and extent of change. These are described as meta-factors because they condition everything – the strategies chosen, selection of people, priorities and style of leadership needed.

Time frames have an important effect on the strategies chosen – in the longer run, more options for strategic action open up – but sometimes managers must deal with critical

Figure 6 ■ The time/change model

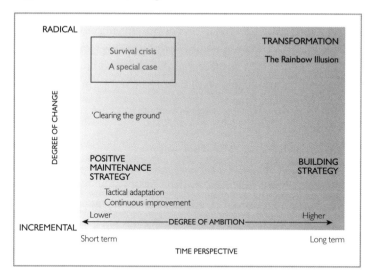

matters in the short term or there will be no longer term. Time can be considered in two ways: how much time is available and how much time will it take?

Extent of change is also crucial. An organisation facing a life-threatening crisis will need rapid and radical treatment, rather like a patient in an emergency department. But once the patient's condition has stabilised, the treatment needs to switch to remedial care to build longer-term health. An environment of continuous crisis, advocated by some radical gurus, simply causes widespread neurosis and failure. The default position for most organisations is continuous innovation and incremental improvement.

There are three generic strategies (see Figure 6):

■ **Crisis management.** This strategy is used where time is short and extensive change is imperative.

■ **Transformation.** Described in the model as the 'rainbow illusion', this strategy is usually appropriate only in the case of start-ups or small organisations.

- **Positive maintenance and building.** Where timescales are
  relatively long but the rate and extent of necessary change
  are small, strategies based on continuous improvement
  and incremental innovation work best. This strategy
  is subdivided into positive maintenance and building,
  depending on the degree of long-term ambition for growth.

Here are some further ideas about when these strategies will
be appropriate:

Crisis management

- Because of past mistakes, neglect, or possibly suddenly
  changing circumstances, such as loss of key people or entry
  of a powerful new competitor, it becomes apparent that
  disaster is nigh. But more often enterprises slide gradually
  down a slippery slope of complacency leading to atrophy
  and only at the last moment do people perceive the
  approach of impending disaster.

- The enterprise is non-viable and will collapse without
  short-term drastic remedial action. In commercial
  organisations the collapse of viability is likely to lead to
  serious loss of market position and a financial crisis, and
  in public services organisations to a collapse in quality of
  service or an unsustainable service/cost relationship.

- The prognosis is that it is imperative to fix the immediate
  problems quickly.

- A healthy outcome is to create the conditions for
  substantial, long-term improvements in performance.

- Unhealthy outcomes are failure to stop the rot or to move
  beyond short-term fixes.

Positive maintenance

- No organisation can afford to stand still. Enterprises
  that do not see the opportunity to engage in ambitious

change at a particular point in their existence still need to pursue innovation, improvement and cost reduction in all that they do. A well-planned and executed process of improvement, affecting many parts of the organisation, is described as a 'positive maintenance' strategy. BMW, an automobile maker, has practised for many years a strategy of incremental innovation that has made its cars among the world's best in terms of drivability and applied technology. Its one excursion into a more radical strategy, the acquisition of Rover, ended in failure. Such relentless attention to detail is sometimes viewed as boring by impatient Anglo-Saxon managers, business gurus and investors.

Building

■ The difference in strategic approach between 'positive maintenance' and 'building' lies in the degree of ambition within an enterprise. A building strategy assumes that the enterprise has a sound business model, is innovative, efficient and on top of its business, and wishes to exploit these strengths to grow. This means adopting a conservative approach to maintaining existing strengths but using this strong base to enter new markets, often in other parts of the world. This strategy has been used successfully by many Japanese and Asian companies.

■ No radical shifts are predicted in the strategic environment which would threaten the fundamentals of the business.

■ The enterprise has built core competencies and an organisation that enable it to be a superior competitor with strengths that cannot easily be replicated by competitors.

■ The leadership has a long-term mindset and a predilection towards incremental growth.

■ The enterprise has a high degree of ambition to enhance the size or scope of the business; this could stretch from achieving a unassailable position in one market to world dominance.

Contingent strategic leadership

The three main change strategies are markedly different and require distinctive leadership behaviours. There are few men or women for all seasons: leaders need to be selected for the circumstances. Failure to do so could result in disaster. However, there seems to be a common misconception that good leaders all have the same characteristics, often described rather vaguely as charismatic, decisive or dynamic. Nothing could be further from the truth.

Thus those in leadership positions or those who select leaders need to be aware that choices will have to be made about which kind of leadership is most appropriate for the circumstances and what kinds of leaders are most likely to be successful. For example, good leaders in crisis conditions are seldom successful when it comes to the long haul and the consistent pursuit of a strategy of incremental improvement. Equally, managers who are temperamentally in favour of an incremental approach to change will probably be inappropriate in a real crisis. Although some managers are flexible and can pursue different strategies in a contingent way, it is unlikely that one person can span the more extreme circumstances. Failure to make important decisions about the appropriate leadership strategies and who is comfortable with them with skill and sensitivity may lead enterprises into deep trouble.

A good psychologist will be able to determine the personality traits needed for different change strategies. Gurnek Bains of YSC, a leading business psychology consultancy, describes the leadership characteristics needed to successfully manage a crisis:

- high energy;
- high impact;

- emotional detachment;

- expressive and communicative;

- hard-headedness;

- capacity to focus on concrete variables that can be affected in the short term;

- impatient, with strong results orientation;

- ability to energise self and the organisation around key, concrete goals;

- capacity to take emotional distance from the organisation;

- capacity to deal harshly with low performers or excess staff;

- high ego needs in terms of impact.

And those suitable for positive maintenance and building strategies:

- ability to bond closely with the organisation;

- concern to create an integrated and cohesive culture;

- relatively low ego needs in terms of profile and impact;

- capacity to develop and follow a conservative long-term vision;

- willingness to work with detail;

- conceptual skills and ability to think about the organisation as a whole;

- ability to address both concrete and tangible and conceptual and soft areas;

- attention to detail, but capacity to integrate specifics against a broader picture;

- consistency and planfulness;

- 'steady hand on the tiller' style of management.

■ psychological conservatism in terms of protecting the core culture, values and purpose of the organisation;

■ interest in growing and expanding the business along conventional performance lines (eg, size, scope of markets, etc);

■ capacity to innovate and adapt in less fundamental areas.

Basket cases

I am generally optimistic about the capacity of organisations and individuals to learn and adapt, which means that most enterprises which have the will to survive and thrive can do so, assuming that they are appropriately staffed and skilfully led. This confidence is at odds with the doctrine of creative destruction that some believe in.

But sometimes my optimism is misplaced. I was once a director of a shipping company that had a collective death wish. Bad relations between management and staff over many decades had bred a deep negativity; nobody was willing to try new things, and management was regarded as a status, not an active role. In the end, it was obviously best to kill off the organisation rather than try to save it.

Sometimes enterprises lose their customer franchise, or changes in technology, fashion or consumer preferences make them deeply unviable. In such cases a kindly death is best. So those involved in leading change have a fundamental decision to make: is it worth saving this organisation, or is euthanasia the best solution?

■ Useful ideas for managing change

Understand the organisation's 'implicit contract'

Individuals and groups of employees have an implicit, often unconscious, contract that influences the effort or type of personal contribution they are willing to make over a sustained period. On one side of this contract is the effort, commitment or personal contribution they are willing to make, and on the other is the bundle of rewards and satisfaction that they perceive the employer is providing. Their perceptions are obviously strongly affected by the comparisons they make with other people. These will be affected not only by current work and personal circumstances but also by prior experiences at work and what they understand the effort/reward relationship to have been in their current organisation up till now.

In the extreme, the unexplained or unconcerned violation of this implicit contract is the most frequent cause of people leaving their job, reducing their effort or sabotaging the plans of their bosses, either blatantly through blocking or subtly through parody and sceptical humour.

Communication at the beginning of a change process therefore needs to provide a clear and compelling rationale for 'why we and, in particular, I have to change'. This communication and all the reinforcing behaviour that goes with it must try to give some indication of a new but equally satisfying implicit contract.

Create a critical mass

Are there sufficient people behaving and apparently thinking differently to be visible and to act as a model for others? Is their collective impact sufficient to overcome existing group norms and social pressure to conform? Some people have much greater influence than others. Do you know who the principal influencers are so that you can make them part of the critical mass at the earliest possible stage? Equally, or perhaps more importantly, do you know who the blockers are – those who will have a negative effect on the change process and whose influence must somehow be neutralised?

Create leverage

Use ordinary events, management processes or the adaptation of systems to create disproportionate effects on behaviour or thinking. For instance, consciously manage the timing and sequencing of events to send particular messages; stack the odds more in favour of acceptable forms of action; make small but significant happenings visible to a wider audience; deliberately design teams to both create their normal outputs and develop the capabilities of the members at minimal extra cost.

Make good use of symbolism

Recognise the strange law of hierarchy that all subordinates tend to assume that all the behaviour of superiors is intentional and has meaning beyond its face value. Senior managers must be careful about how they behave, because what they say and do will be closely observed and interpreted by staff.

Provide lots of reinforcement

Most organisations are better at punishing than rewarding. Even where they give careful attention to the so-called reward system, it can often have significant demotivational effects on a high proportion of people. Reinforcement in some contexts is not by financial reward, but in the context of change, more subtle messages of approval or appreciation – or even just interest – seem to have a more powerful impact.

Don't try to tackle values and beliefs head-on

Because the deepest factors affecting work behaviour (ie, values and beliefs) are often hidden and private, it is inadvisable to attempt to work directly on these at the beginning of a change process. There is strong evidence that change in behaviour leads to changes in attitudes and eventually to changes in values and beliefs, not the reverse.

When people are feeling reasonably secure, understand why change is necessary, have begun to change their behaviour and are prepared to trust those around them, it is possible to bring the unspoken to the surface and have discussions that allow individuals to examine and question their values, recognise the link to behaviour and begin the long-term process of adaptation along with others.

Final thoughts

Make change natural

Much rubbish has been written about change. A fad of the 1990s was culture change. Many an enterprise employed expensive consultants to help them, not realising that changing a culture is subject to 'obliquity' – cultures cannot be predictably changed by addressing them head on.

Healthy change tends to be natural, even invisible. It is the organisation adapting to the environment around it and seeking to learn and innovate. It might be called organic change and is the default state of healthy enterprises.

The need to make extensive and urgent changes is usually the result of dysfunction: organisations getting cut off from reality; leaders pursuing synthetic strategies divorced from reality or grand plans, deals, mergers and acquisitions.

Crisis is not a default change position

Once a crisis has been weathered, it is crucial to move towards a healthy default position, lengthening time horizons and building steadily for a long-term future. Once in a blue moon, opportunities arise to revolutionise what enterprises do or how they do it. Leaders with vision matched by realism and determination may be able to grasp such opportunities and infuse their vision in the wider organisation. But there have been many more failed transformation attempts than successful ones.

Design and implement an improvement plan

The five-stage process outlined in this section aims to help managers raise the level of achievement in their organisations.

Stage 1: Forming hypotheses, scoping the job, preparing the ground

The first stage of a full cycle of improvement and change will determine the shape of subsequent programmes. It is important before starting to gain an understanding of the scope and size of the tasks ahead and the questions below are designed to elicit ideas for this. The questioning process should be widely shared and gather information from a number of internal and external sources. One approach is for small teams to take soundings from different sources and levels inside the enterprise and from outside (there are many well-documented cases of enterprises getting into trouble because their leaders listened only to voices that reinforced their prejudices).

Questions to consider

- Are we ready and willing to begin a long-term process of improvement? Is there sufficient support for what might be an uncomfortable change process? Are we realistic about our strengths and (particularly) weaknesses?

- What are we dissatisfied about? What are the problems that concern us? How big do they seem to be? How much time do we have to act? What is the size of the gaps between the current position and what might be a sustainable and satisfactory one?

- What problems have emerged? Do we need to dig beneath the problems to get to the underlying causes of malaise?

- Do we have sufficient and reliable quantified information – financial and operational? What about more qualitative information – employee attitudes, customer opinions, stakeholder views? Do the quantified and qualitative information stack up consistently? What don't we know that we would like to find out? Generally, how might we go about this?

- Does the initial prognosis suggest that we face a crisis and need to act urgently and make extensive changes? Or is it an opportunity to keep improving our business, taking advantage of our existing strengths, innovating and/or growing organically?

- What are we satisfied with? What do we do so well that it constitutes a strength that distinguishes our enterprise? What might we need to conserve and strengthen, ensuring that we do not 'throw the baby out with the bathwater' in a change process. What are the manifestations of strength, described in quantified and qualitative terms? Do we have external benchmarks to compare ourselves against? Are our strengths relevant to the changing environment? Are we improving rapidly enough to keep up with customer/client demands or competitor actions?

- Is the climate right for change? Do we know enough to make an accurate assessment? Who/where might resistance come from? How will we initiate investigations? Who will sponsor? Who will lead? Who will be involved? Do we need external support to provide expertise and objectivity?

- Who do we need to communicate with and brief about our objectives? Who do we need to conduct negotiations with or influence? How do we select people to interview or speak to in order to gather data? What might constitute a valid sample? Who can we meet in groups, or individually and privately? Who do we need to contact outside the organisation? Who will do this? How many people will we need to meet?

- What timescales are we thinking of? When might we start/ finish the initial investigations? How will we 'feel the pulse' and make initial assessments of what is emerging? How will investigations be co-ordinated? How will the various investigating teams stay in touch with each other? What structure of interim reports and discussions should we create to ensure a coherent overall process? How will sponsors stay in touch so that they can respond appropriately to the emerging picture and continue to show interest and commitment? What will we do if emerging information shows a different picture from the one expected?

Stage 2: Investigation and building a picture

This is a crucial stage. The quality of the enquiry process will determine the effectiveness of subsequent actions; and a well-designed and executed investigation will build foundations for commitment and participation by the wider organisational population. In one enterprise that I worked with as a consultant, this stage of the process revealed that the majority of staff were rightly committed to a devolved front line while senior management wanted to suck authority upwards. Top managers (their superiors) were persuaded of the validity of the frontline case, which was well received, and a major change programme got off to a flying start led by new senior managers.

This stage is best managed as a rolling process, using data unearthed to progressively build hypotheses that will form an ever richer picture of what is going on and what actions might be appropriate. The word 'picture' is used deliberately because what emerges from investigation and questioning is likely to be in many forms, some hard-edged and quantitative, some much more akin to a real picture or vision of what could be. In any case, words are likely to be as important as numbers, if not more so. Descriptions of the situation and views as to what needs to be done can be evocative – accounting figures are best used to reinforce a case made verbally.

It is important to encourage a vigorous process of dialectic and challenge, as this can guard against hasty or superficial conclusions.

Questions to consider

Process

■ Who needs to be on board to enable change and improvement to work? Are there problems at the top levels? Will corporate politics get in the way and how might we prepare the ground politically? Do we know the agendas and concerns of key individuals and groups of people? Might we need to spend energy and time preparing the ground for change, possibly weeding out potential sources of resistance?

■ How are investigation teams to be configured? What skills do we want the teams to have? Who will select those involved and how will they be prepared? Who will be in each team? What is the overall structure of the investigation: who will be sponsors, who will co-ordinate the overall effort, how many teams doing what? How will teams be supported? Will external helpers be attached to each team? What kinds and how many external helpers will we need? What will be their roles: what will they do and not do? What kind of information do we wish to elicit from outside the enterprise? Who will seek it from where?

- What are the questions that we wish to investigate? Where will the information come from? What are the interviewing schedules? Who will organise people to be seen? When will lists be available?

- When do we start the process? When will the first interim reviews take place? When do we wish to finish? What is the schedule for discussion and consideration of findings?

- What will be the structure of formal and informal meetings to share views and impressions between investigators? Who will keep top managers in touch? Will any top managers participate in the investigations, and if so, how?

- What will we do to ensure adequate discussion and dialectic during the process to provide richness and challenge for those involved? How will we deal with differences of view as the investigations progress?

- What messages will we need to get across before the investigations commence and as they progress? What will be done to allay the fears of those who may think they will be negatively affected? How do we assure staff that they have a significant role to play and that their views will be respected and where appropriate acted upon?

- As the time for pulling the threads together approaches, how will we prepare for reporting to top management and how will we do it? Do some top people need to be briefed separately before a top team meets? What do we want from top managers? How will permission to act and move forward be granted? How will participants be informed about what is emerging and its implications? Do we wish to arrange special feedback seminars or meetings for those who have participated in the process?

More substantive issues

■ What is the cost of major activities that span the organisation such as planning, reporting and financial control or human resources policies and procedures? Do they add more value than cost? What is the cost of the corporate infrastructure? Can its activities, resources and costs be assessed in relation to its value-adding contributions? What are the relationships between overhead costs and those of frontline activities? Can they be justified in terms of added value?

■ Where and who are our key people for the medium-term and long-term? Are they good enough to take the enterprise forward on a track of continuous improvement? Are there enough of them? Are there excellent people at the front line of the organisation? How do we know? Are our top people sufficiently in touch with them to make an intelligent assessment? What is being done to refresh and develop our talent. Is this enough?

■ What is the emerging big picture? Who is responsible for pulling it together? What are the components of the picture – financial shortfalls, organisational strengths and weaknesses, significant divergences of view in different parts and levels, big changes and improvements that may need to be made? Does the picture indicate radical or progressive change? What do people believe about timescales? What is good and must be preserved at all costs? What is dysfunctional and must be rectified at all costs? What facets of the business need the most improvement?

◼ Stage 3: Reflection

This is an important step in building learning into the improvement process. The temptation to take piecemeal action should be avoided, unless there is a full-blooded crisis. Allowing time and space for reflection and thought enables the views of many to be sought, different scenarios and possibilities to be considered, and external perspectives to be examined.

This is a time for creativity and lateral thinking and an important opportunity for learning, before deciding on courses of action. It can also be an important way of getting a wide variety of people committed to change. They will know that their views have been sought and valued.

Typically, a process of reflection might cover:

◼ what the investigators believe to be the important issues;

◼ differences of perspective from the investigation, anomalies and conflicting views – and reconciliation of differences;

◼ finding common themes and ascribing significance to them;

◼ the overall meaning of what has been found – what is most important, what is most urgent, what can be done easily without delay;

◼ options for action;

◼ priorities and timescales.

It can include seminars and group discussions in which the information assembled through an investigation is considered and the views of a wide range of people are heard. If appropriate, external perspectives should be sought. It is important that the way in which these activities are conducted encourages strong challenge and questioning and exploration of different views and options.

Questions to consider

- What insights can we derive from the experiences of others and the relevant literature, models and constructs?

- Who will be involved in considering the outputs of the investigation phase? How can a representative range of opinions be assembled? If the participants are from different status levels, how will the views of all be given adequate weight?

- How much of this phase should be conducted in plenary sessions and how much in smaller groups? What will be the relationship between the two? For example, will the reflection stage be initiated with plenary sessions and then participants split into groups, coming back for plenary review? What are the outputs of group sessions to be? How will views be captured and reported?

- Is it appropriate to invite external participants and experts to play a part at this stage? Where should they come from? Will the sessions be facilitated from inside or outside?

- How many different perspectives are there? Are they capable of being reconciled? How might we go about doing this?

- Are there issues that are still not clear? Do we know enough to proceed to action? What more do we need to know to be safe in our decisions? Or do we proceed with a tentative action programme, expecting to learn as we go along whether we are correct in our assumptions?

- Can we now confirm the big issues emerging from the investigations and our reflections?

- What seem to be the most important or most urgent issues to address? What are the timescales we will need to work with?

- What do we need to do to clear the ground for action?

Stage 4: Planning and action

It may take a long time to get to action, but careful planning and wide involvement will make implementation of changes easier. There are marked differences around the world in the value placed on careful planning and preparation before acting. In some cultures there is an impatient rush to action – sometimes any action; in others there is a reluctance to act before proper consideration, involvement and planning. The approach proposed here tends more towards careful preparation and planning, but recognises that it is almost impossible to assemble all the information needed for a perfect plan, and that things will change and new learning will occur as a result of acting.

The planning phase involves determining what programmes of action and projects will be initiated, how they will be co-ordinated and led, who will be involved, and how the wider organisation will be engaged in change. How to cope with obstacles and resistance, what aspects of the current organisation will be preserved and protected and what will be changed must be considered. But the main work will be preparing, initiating and monitoring action projects. This will entail scoping the objectives and deciding who will lead, who will participate, how the overall programme will be sequenced and how each project will be communicated to those who will be affected.

Almost inevitably there will be casualties along the way, and decisions will have to be made about how to handle them to avoid arousing bad feelings and resistance on the part of those whose co-operation is needed for success. It should be made clear who has responsibility, authority and oversight and how the project leaders will report on progress and problems.

Progress (including progress for each project) and milestones will need to be defined. Progress can be measured against the project objectives and, at a deeper level, by checking that the anticipated longer-term results expected are being achieved. It is important to remember that progress will be more assured if reflection and learning possibilities are built into the process for each project and for the overall programme, so that the habit of building learning into the fabric of the culture becomes established.

Questions to consider

- How will the most senior people signify their support?

- What will be the key projects? What issues will they address?

- Can we develop a phased programme of projects that will address the issues and that can be represented in a form (possibly critical path diagram or Gantt chart) that is clear and understandable to a wide range of people?

- Who will lead each project? Who will be involved with each project team? Who will directly participate? Whose support and occasional involvement will be necessary?

- Do we have access to the skills and perspectives required to do a thorough job?

- How will each project be reviewed? Who/how will the overall programme be co-ordinated? Can we specify project milestones to enable progress to be assessed?

- What are we going to communicate to people inside (and outside) the organisation. What media will we use? How can we be sure that everybody is properly involved and communicated with?

- What is our time horizon? Will some projects take longer than others? Are projects interrelated or interdependent? What is likely to be the critical path between them?

- What means will be used to assess the success or failure of each project and the whole process? Can performance reporting be built in as a regular part of the whole process?

- Is there scope for experimentation and trying new things to test ways forward?

- What processes will be installed to ensure that important learning is registered and built into future actions? Who will be responsible for making sure that this happens?

Stage 5: Evaluation

The means to assess whether actions are having the desired effect should be built into the planning and action process. Evaluation has two dimensions:

- Detecting signs that behaviour is changing in ways that are likely to be beneficial. Direct observation and informal feedback through networks of leaders and activists are likely to be the best ways of doing this.

- Hard evidence of performance improvement in quantified forms. Some data will be financial as measured through the accounting process, and some may refer to performance in the market. It is important that such data are fed to the people who are most closely involved with working on improvements. For example, the customer complaints department of a food company assiduously collected complaints about packing errors and sent them to the production department, with little apparent impact. But when a specific programme of improvement was introduced for packing staff and customer feedback delivered directly to the production line, the effect on motivation and on defects was dramatic.

The overall process of performance improvement should be subject to formal review at appropriate intervals to keep the whole organisation closely in touch with progress and problems. The same information should be available to all levels in the organisation. Each improvement project should be reviewed in the same way. It is important that both progress and problems are logged and communicated to a wide audience, so that there is widespread involvement in the improvement process.

Continuous learning and improvement

Learning should be built into the normal processes of the organisation as well as those of specific projects to avoid the risk of spurts of change followed by relative stasis and even atrophy. Change that is sporadic and jerky can be unsettling and destabilising.

The following processes have been tried and have worked well:

- Keeping planning and review processes open-ended, thus encouraging discussion and exploration before closing in on decisions and action. A planning process that encourages full description of the operating and competitive environments, together with an evaluation of issues, and then concludes with a description of strategic and tactical options can be far better than one which results in fully formed proposals made before there is room for joint review. Thus a two-phase approach can work well: first scenario-building and description of options for discussion, then agreement and preparation of the final plan integrating different planning dimensions.

- Most business plans have financial and market dimensions, and they may also take into account economic and technological factors. Too seldom do they integrate constructive thinking about the capability of the organisation and staff to deliver the plan. Business plans should always incorporate an assessment of organisational strengths and weaknesses and a review of talent and potential, identifying gaps and issues needing to be addressed. This will help highlight actions that need to be taken to reshape an organisation to fit the challenges it faces, which may involve major development and recruitment programmes, the identification of acquisition targets and the redeployment of senior managers across different businesses.

■ Establishing continuous communication and dialogue across the organisation. The best form of business intelligence usually lies near to an enterprise's operating front line. The best form of communication is that which occurs easily and naturally between people who know and trust each other. All too often senior management can become trapped in their corporate fortresses. All too frequently they only meet others on their terms in their offices. Not long ago many top managers had separate entrances to their offices. Such segregation can have damaging effects on enterprises; it is well known that physical isolation increases the risks of people developing negative fantasies about 'them'. Top managers who cannot mix easily and naturally with their colleagues at any level are lacking a critical skill and are also likely to cut themselves off from crucial intelligence, thus diminishing their effectiveness and relevance.

■ Making external exploration and informal benchmarking a way of life. This can be built into planning, performance improvement and development programmes. For example:
  – Instead of sending production staff on courses at the local college, one company invited college staff to work with them to address a range of quality and sampling problems. As a result, the production staff learned some new techniques and college lecturers learned how to apply theoretical constructs to real problems.
  – A business academic invited to work with a group of senior managers found himself not lecturing to managers in a classroom, but facilitating a live investigation. After this experience of reality, he confessed that he had never been so challenged.

–   A business academic was invited to work with several management teams on their organisational problems. After the top teams of several divisions presented their business and organisation, the professor interrogated them, and managers worked with him to think through the issues that had emerged and how to deal with them effectively.

–   A board invited peers from non-competing companies to explore a range of issues that were felt to be common. Through the course of a day, in a confidential environment, delicate issues were honestly discussed to mutual benefit.

–   A multinational team of general managers, having thought through the competencies needed to attain high achievement, visited other organisations to explore how they addressed problems that may not have appeared to be similar. It soon became clear that logistics problems in food retailing and distribution and delivery issues in aggregates and road-building needed similar systems solutions.

■   Building real-life exploration and action into learning and development programmes. In several action-learning programmes for senior general managers, participants are encouraged to conduct an in-depth review of their own businesses and then work with other members of their set to work up a performance improvement plan. The role of fellow set members is to offer constructive challenge and new perspectives to the subjects' thinking, leading to the involvement of others in the business in planning and action. The most important issue is to avoid the separation of learning and development from real life, to try where possible to bring external resources and expertise into the enterprise to help address real problems in real time. Too often managers and other staff are sent away for training and then have to find ways of applying their learning back

home. This has been shown to be an extremely ineffective
way of deploying learning to improve performance.

▣ Identifying internal centres of excellence, making them
widely known, and encouraging internal dialogue and visits
to discuss experience and applications. One organisation
I worked for published an internal directory of experience
and expertise and encouraged people who had special
skills to be used in multiple locations to assist in problem
diagnosis and problem solving. This was launched across
the world by an internal team of three people who acted as
a sort of 'telephone exchange' to put people in touch with
each other.

▣ Building customers/clients into internal reviews and
development processes. Ensuring that customer/client
feedback reaches all levels of the organisation. Feeding
customer opinion, reaction and complaints directly to
the people who can immediately do something about it.
Encouraging top managers to spend time working at the
front line in operations, sales and customer service.

Appendix
'The happy coincidence' at work

Some of the greatest enterprises of the nineteenth century were founded by men with strong moral, religious and humanistic beliefs. They believed that basing their businesses on the foundations of staff well-being, customer value and strong ethics was crucial to success – and highly successful they did indeed become. This phenomenon became known as 'the happy coincidence'. Such enterprises included Unilever, the John Lewis Partnership and firms founded by Quakers such as Rowntree and Cadbury.

In the rush for instant success and maximum financial returns, many in the modern world have forgotten what underpinned these firms' success, and this has led to corporate underperformance and failure, staff exploitation, customer rip-offs and grossly disparate personal rewards.

The following profiles show aspects of 'the happy coincidence' at work in companies of different sizes in different industries.

▦ Profile of a high-achieving large enterprise

The Group, as I shall call it, was founded before the Second World War by an entrepreneur. It has grown to be a major enterprise with worldwide sales in excess of £10 billion, generated by a wide range of businesses operating on every continent. It has a market capitalisation of over £6 billion and borrowings of less than £1 billion.

It is still mainly family owned but some 40 per cent of its shares are publicly quoted. Its public faces are mainly through its consumer and industrial brands, rather than the Group. Family ownership is exercised through an investment trust with professional investment management and family trustees. There is also a large charitable and philanthropic trust that supports a wide range of causes.

The following profile is derived from an in-depth discussion with a director.

Values

We believe in modesty and keeping a low public profile. Manifestations of ego and publicity-seeking behaviour are strongly discouraged. We do not do ventures driven by personal egos. This probably comes from the values of the founders. We are not cheap and we do not pursue the lowest cost; we believe in creating value for customers, staff and the company and despise waste and flamboyant excess. We are financially conservative, but have grown steadily. We are not subject to pressure to grow endlessly from the investment markets, which in my view causes many companies to hire high-ego, growth-obsessed risk takers who lead their companies into difficulty and sometimes ruin.

There are no special privileges in this company – the top people travel club class for long distance and in the back of the plane for shorter journeys. We stay in moderately priced hotels. When we moved offices to a prime city-centre location, there was a long period of adjustment and some feelings of guilt about the cost of it all. We do not have big offices with flash furniture.

We are not overintellectual: we believe in keeping it as simple as possible. We don't follow fashions: for example, we are quite diversified in a world where the investors' mantra is focus. We can ignore the pressures of the executive fashion industry and simply rely on people who know their businesses well.

We practise high engagement: the small number of people in the corporate office travel incessantly and maintain close personal contact with those who run the operating companies. Taken together, these are the key people in our Group. We strongly believe in 'getting mud on our boots', so corporate staff not only travel to subsidiaries' offices but also get out into the field to see where it really happens. This strongly challenges corporate managers to be relevant and able to add value to the operations. There is no place to hide in the corporate office.

The Group operates through its values and the relationships that have developed over time between a cadre of 15 or so corporate managers and about 100 operating business heads. We have grown up together and know each other well. We believe in dialogue, openness and doing the right thing for the good of the business. This means that if things go wrong, the dialogue must be rapid and the action taken must be in the medium- or longer-term interests of the business. We punish hiding the truth or concealment in the belief that it causes bad long-term problems and undermines trust. People have been summarily fired for concealment and self-serving behaviour.

We do long term. This is liberating for someone like me who has spent a long time in publicly quoted companies. For example, we have invested substantially in a venture in China. The key aspects of this are that we are investing in building a complete regional infrastructure to produce, manufacture and distribute a new product. This is complex and time-consuming, and we estimate it will take 15 years to reach fruition and generate respectable returns. From my experience, no UK publicly quoted company would be able to do this without significant investor resistance.

Planning and strategy

We believe strongly in making commitments and doing our best to meet them. We call them 'contracts', but they are psychological commitments, not written documents. A contract is a jointly reached commitment forged through corporate and operating management working together to craft the strategy and plans for a business. The main elements are a strategy – what the business intends to do over a period, usually of three years; a budget, which contains the financial and operating performance commitments; and an agreement on the capital and revenue expenditure requirements to meet the strategy. Associated with the strategy is a plan to ensure that the business is adequately resourced with the appropriate people, in terms of numbers and quality.

Performance management

This is managed jointly by the CEO, corporate staff and the business heads. There is a small corporate performance function that works directly for the CEO, not the finance director. If things go wrong and a business is going to miss its commitments in market, operating or financial terms, it is mandatory that those running the business should signal this as soon as they suspect matters are going off course. Then we can work together to decide what to do. This entails an absolute commitment to doing the right thing for the business. 'Doing the right thing' entails considering the longer-term implications of any short-term actions and, if necessary, taking a short-term hit to ensure the longer-term health of the enterprise. Providing it doesn't become a repetitive habit, people are not sanctioned for raising their hands and giving early warning of problems. What is totally unacceptable is trying to disguise or hide problems – that would break the trust implied in the contract.

Corporately we use earnings per share (EPS) as a key long-term performance measure. This works well for us because we don't issue or buy back shares very much, so it can be a stable measure. At the operating level, we like to track cash generation and longer-term (five year) value creation regarding the cost of capital invested.

Selection and appointment

Selecting new people to join the Group at senior levels is a lengthy process that involves prospective joiners meeting a wide cross-section of family and non-family members. I would describe it as taking many subjective impressions and bringing them together to make an objective judgement about whether to select or not. Another perspective is that of joining a family. Some people are completely amazed by the experience, but what is clear is that the candidate and the Group know a great deal about each other before any specific proposals and offers are made. In my view, this is a sensible process, as we expect the association to be a long one with strong mutual commitment.

Reward and incentives

We are not high payers (most of us could earn maybe four or five times more with quoted companies and certainly with private equity-owned enterprises). What holds us together is the sense of shared values, the excitement and commitment that come from strong psychological ownership of the Group and its businesses, and the sense of destiny generated by the fact that we are moving forward together. There is considerable scope for advancement in most of our business areas and some can forge an international career – although we are mainly committed to having indigenous managers in most geographical regions. This seems to be a stronger binding force than money alone – and I guess that people who are money or ego driven don't join, and certainly don't stay. I personally feel a strong sense of loyalty and commitment to the people I have grown with over the past ten years and have no desire to work anywhere else.

We have variable rewards as well as basic pay. These are constructed on a 'line of sight' basis; in other words, incentive rewards are paid for the unit for which executives are responsible. The structure of these plans is as simple as possible and we do not have any share-related rewards. This means that we can avoid the complex plans and elaborate governance structures that seem to me to plague the quoted sector.

Structures and organisation

There are three elements in the company: the family investment trust; the board, led by the chairman; and the operating group, led by the chief executive. There is minimal hierarchy, so those who manage operating businesses have frequent contact with corporate managers. The investment trust has family members as trustees and is professionally staffed. In effect it is the investment bank for the Group. The chairman is not a member of the family and one of his roles is to hold the ring between the family trust and the operating group. Another is to ensure that the interests of all key stakeholders are properly considered when important decisions are made.

We have had three external chairmen in the past ten years, two of whom had a long-term association with the Group before assuming the chair. The most recent appointee came from another family-related group. The process of appointing him took a long time – many meetings, lunches and dinners with individuals and small groups. Then we took soundings, only acting when there was near-consensus that the individual had the right skills and, more importantly, the right values. This meant that what might have been a traumatic initial period of working together was considerably eased.

Family business

As a family-owned group, there are obviously sensitive issues to be managed. But there are strong values, principles and practices that have become deeply rooted. The most important is the practice of encouraging all younger members of the direct family to become involved early with the business in ways that will help them to realise how the family's wealth is created – by making and selling things. Thus they will all have spent time working at the front line before they have to decide on their careers. This discourages any sense of privilege or special status. Another is to ensure that there is always a blend of professional and family members involved in the running of the Group. The tripartite arrangement of board, family investment trust and executive is an effective safeguard against any one element getting big ideas and taking unacceptable risks.

Risks and threats

One risk is that a major part of the business goes belly-up. We try to guard against this becoming a life-threatening event by preserving the balance of businesses that have different risk profiles and behave differently through economic cycles. We have enough businesses in staple everyday products that are fairly recession-proof. Another is, of course, succession. This is not a short-term problem but will in time have to be handled carefully. We have survived three changes of generation, and I think we are much helped by the strength and depth of the all-pervasive culture that binds both family and non-family members. Our last CEO was non-family and we hardly noticed, because he was a long-serving manager and committed to the values.

Profile of YSC, a high-achieving smaller company

Narrated by Don Young, from interviews with a cross-section of directors and staff.

I was one of the founders of YSC, my (now) wife, then Charlotte Chambers, was another and the third, Peter Samuel, died some years back. The two current leaders of the practice, Gurnek Bains and Ken Rowe, were part of the founding team.

YSC is a London-based business psychology consultancy with offices in the United States, Mexico, Brazil, Hong Kong, India, Australia and South Africa and associates in the Netherlands and Germany. It is planning to open an office in Singapore. It employs 90 consultants (65 full-time equivalents), has 60 support staff and in 2011 billed more than £20 million.

It has grown steadily since 1990 when it was founded, failing to grow in only two of its twenty-plus years. Its clients include many of the largest British companies, and it is growing organically in most of the countries where it has offices. YSC works at the higher end of the business psychology market, and has an assessment process that depends largely on the skills and perceptions of consultants. Its roots therefore lie in clinical psychology – it is not dependent on tests or 'psychometrics', rather basing its practice on understanding individuals as a whole, working in specific contexts. This approach is particularly suited to senior executives, many of whom dislike being tested. For YSC, the clients are both the organisation for which it is working and the individuals it is assessing and counselling. This, as will be seen later, has beneficial marketing implications.

The story of this successful enterprise is told through the eyes of people whose experience stretches from one to twenty years, from seasoned consultants to relative newcomers. It is not possible to describe YSC in conventional hierarchical terms because its hierarchy is based on experience, skills, client relationships and the ability to bring in work. Despite this, there is a group of people called 'directors' and two individuals who are most respected and influential because of their abilities and experience. This small group of long-serving senior consultants own most of the shares in the company.

Finally, YSC is one of the few corporate psychology companies to have lasted the course. Many others have 'blown up' or failed.

The story

YSC was conceived by three senior corporate managers, Peter Samuel, Charlotte Chambers and Don Young who, having reached the age of fifty or so, wanted to start a new phase of their working lives. Gestation was lengthy, starting with 'wouldn't it be good if' conversations and gradually closing in on a notion of what 'our business' might be. There was no formal plan or strategy (nor has there ever been). We each knew what we were good at, developed a mutual understanding of each other's complementary skills, and agreed to build a practice on our strengths. Before we started, I produced a concept paper that laid out a number of important precepts:

- The overriding priority would be service to clients.

- We would not indulge in formal marketing or selling, instead using our networks and client referral to gain business.

- We would start with a minimal cost base with low initial pay and no perks.

- There would be little formal hierarchy – the demands of client projects would override any notion of seniority.

- Administration would be kept to an absolute minimum.

- We would leave some space for our own development.

The first opportunity (or stroke of luck) that came our way – even before we started – was when we got word that a large American consultancy with a London office was in the process of disintegration and that, because of their dissatisfaction with their Chicago-based top management, two very bright consultants (the aforementioned Gurnek Bains and Ken Rowe) were interested in joining whatever it was we were setting up. It was a simple decision to hire them, and some of their clients came with them. Then a former colleague who was a director of a large electricity utility that was approaching privatisation asked for help and advice on how to cope with massive changes in the business and the organisation. Thus began a five-year relationship that benefited both parties greatly.

These two strokes of 'luck', supplemented by the fact that each of the founders invested a small amount in the business and all involved brought sufficient business from their erstwhile organisations, meant that we started cash positive and we were able to live from the income the business generated.

The first year saw healthy revenues and several new clients. But it also saw the first crisis – two of the founders had a monumental falling out. This was overcome thanks to some careful mediation from the third and the fact that each of us had a different area of practice and so could work apart, but it made things difficult. However, more new clients were attracted to the business, requiring the recruitment of several consultants.

As our experience grew, it became apparent that some aspects of YSC's practice were not viable. In particular, we were head to head with consulting giants like McKinsey in some facets of our work, especially strategy and organisation. More seriously, two of the original founders wanted to move on to other work. This spelled impending doom – or did it? Another opportunity? Hard to see, but maybe there was a glimmer of hope.

We engaged in an intense rolling discussion about possible futures, and the conviction grew that YSC could thrive as a specialist high-quality provider of business psychology services. A crucial part of this emerging consensus was that YSC's practice could extend beyond individual assessment to a range of other streams of psychology-related work, such as assessing whole management cadres, team building, coaching and survey-feedback.

This caused serious disagreement, but eventually there was a dénouement, with those who wanted a wider-based practice winning. This led to the appointment of Bains and Rowe as joint managing directors and me as chair. So, out of life-threatening problems and disputes emerged a strategic direction that has lasted 20 years, under the direction of Bains and Rowe, who luckily had a deep symbiotic relationship, despite being very different characters. Charlotte Chambers went on to set up her own business and I eventually joined the board of Redland, a company facing great difficulties.

The next 15 years saw continuous organic growth and a rapid expansion of the practice internationally. The main constraint on growth was the ability to recruit and induct new consultants of the required intellectual calibre and with personal profiles that would enable them to find their way into an organisation that had a distinctive culture. Outsiders who were wedded to snappy decision-making, systematic and orderly working and clear hierarchy have constantly predicted collapse and doom – but somehow the apparently chaotic ship continued to weather economic storms. The first finance director to be hired had a set model of how a company should run in an orderly fashion – and left in short order. Eventually an individual was found who had the flexibility of mind and the social skills required to worm his way through an apparently impenetrable jungle of resistance to order and bring cash management under some semblance of control. His legacy has been invaluable, and his successor of equal calibre.

Built on the foundations of top-class business psychology, very bright staff, informal organisation that is intensely client focused and high employee engagement, YSC has grown into one of the world's leading consultancies in its field. Most of its growth has been 'viral', and it is still the case that most new business comes from word of mouth and a constantly extending network of senior individuals who have found YSC's assessment and feedback personally valuable.

YSC today

The following insights into the nature of YSC come from a number of interviews with consultants, some of the most interesting being with newer employees:

- It's not easy to join, the process of recruitment can last a long time. It seems more like joining a family, but the encounters pre-recruitment were very stimulating if a bit frustrating.

- On joining, I found everybody very welcoming and friendly. Several senior staff went out of their way to act as guides to how it all worked and the induction programme was useful, but in the end you have to find your own way to getting work. The introduction to YSC's assessment methods is long and intensive and I did not feel able to work on my own for more than six months – and I have a masters in psychology. Once I was free to 'go solo', I felt a great sense of responsibility towards the individual I was assessing – and to YSC.

- It takes quite a long time to realise that in essence YSC is an internal market led by senior consultants. Junior consultants have to work hard and make themselves visible to seniors to be included in the most interesting projects. Those who find that difficult receive support and counselling. There is an element of competition offset by the fact that everybody without exception will go out of the way to help if you ask. The skill levels and quality of practice of the more experienced people are quite awe-inspiring, so I have a lot to aim for. Also the very nature of the work is highly motivational – we are there to help big organisations, but more important, we can have a profound effect on individuals. The work itself provides a lot of meaning for consulting staff.

- I recognise your description of the founding values of YSC – client focus, informal organisation based on personal relationships, lack of formal hierarchy (although there is no doubt about who the bosses are). They are there by expertise, contacts and merit – and they are very accessible, when they're not frantically busy.

- All in all, the organisation is very flexible; able to respond to new challenges and (just) able to service a high workload from clients.

- I see growing pressures to become more systematic in how we organise work, especially how we co-ordinate international offices to meet client demands. We are more systematic in how we manage finances and especially cash – it seems to have sunk in that our pay and dividends are dependent on having the cash to pay for them. But most of the adaptive responses have come from people and client experiences, not systems or formal processes. The early stages of internationalisation were based on 'who wants to go and set up an office', not highly planned moves. But there are now co-ordinating roles for research, international management, new office development, consultant development and finance. Target setting is informal, but there are pressures to perform with clients. I have not sensed any direct financial targets – it's more to do with the quantity and quality of consulting work.

- I would describe the internal functioning of the organisation as 'conscious chaos', because it may appear to be disorderly but everybody including administrative staff has personal 'maps' of how it works and how to get things done. This is helped by the fact that the vast majority of staff are long-serving. YSC doesn't lose a lot of people.

- The real glue in YSC is relationships, in many cases lasting friendships. The friendship and trust that it engenders enable us to achieve alignment of purpose without very much formal planning or systems. We do have strategies; for example: 'From local to global' and 'From success to significance'. These strategies are the subject of intense participation and discussion involving many people, so that they understand what lies behind them and bend their efforts to achieving them.

▓ A bedrock of getting things done in YSC is the mutual respect and friendly relationships between consultants and support staff. Possibly the fact that about 65 per cent of YSC's employees are bright women has a positive impact on the climate.

▓ The friendly culture is reinforced by a commitment to the individuals and client organisations that we serve. Everybody knows that we can help or harm people through our work, and this engenders a great sense of responsibility.

▓ As an employer, YSC pays all its staff well, provides an enjoyable working environment, and gives longer-serving staff sabbaticals provided they use the time to develop ideas and themselves. It has won a number of awards for the quality of its London office facilities and working climate.

YSC – the future

It appears that YSC can continue to grow organically based on its fundamental practice model, supplemented by complementary lines of business in staff survey-feedback and other related fields. There is still ample scope for international development. One big issue is independence.

Many approaches from larger consultancy businesses – some of them very attractive financially – have been turned away because of a conviction that the clash of cultures between YSC and any new owners would be destructive. Similarly, investigations of the possibility of flotation on the stock market have been halted on the grounds that external investors would have difficulty in understanding the nature of the business and organisation.

But there is a looming issue – or perhaps an opportunity. On the horizon is another generational handover period that must be handled carefully in order to secure the future. Only time will tell whether this turns out to be an opportunity or a problem, but YSC has had an excellent track record so far.

YSC is an organisation that runs on a powerful blend of friendship, supportive relationships and mutual trust among able people dedicated to serving clients as individuals and organisations. The meaning and satisfaction derived from this mixture (and good financial rewards) enable the company to operate, set strategic direction, adapt and grow without the need for heavy formal systems or bureaucracy.

The main pillar that supports the company – friendship – would be frowned on by the financial community and many others. Everybody in YSC seems to be passionately committed to the enterprise – and financial markets want management to be 'independent' of their organisations and therefore committed to them. For this reason, it is hard to imagine that a merger with another company or a stock-market flotation, introducing investors who are unlikely to understand such a unique organisation, would do anything but undermine and eventually destroy YSC, which succeeds because of the animal it is.

YSC in its own way matches most of the criteria defining high achievers that were unearthed by André de Waal:

■ **Management and organisation quality**, which encompasses inclusive behaviour, lack of social distance and high engagement in the wider organisation.

■ **Openness and action orientation**, which includes continuous internal dialogue, openness to adaptive change and experimentation.

■ **Long-term orientation**, which includes financial conservatism, investment for improvement, growing their own staff and managers, and sustainable relationships with customers.

- **Culture of continuous improvement**, including progressive innovation of products and practices.

- **Workforce quality**, including suitability for task, dedication to results, high support and continuous learning.

But in the end, it is an organisation built on the relationships between a bright group of people and their close interactions with clients. YSC encompasses many of the characteristics of high achievers, but is unique in its practice model, its founding and continuing values and its people. It is therefore hard to copy.

Profile of Value Partnership

Value Partnership (VP) was founded in 1998 by Simon Court and his wife Jane, with a little help from me and Nickie Fonda, who previously ran her own consulting practice. Court had been a consultant at YSC. He was not a qualified psychologist, and believed that YSC's focus on psychology would provide him with an opportunity to set up on his own. This he did with the blessing of YSC's seniors, and he was able to start his business with two YSC clients.

From the start, they saw the firm as a family venture, their 'family' including the first partner, Geoff Rogers, who joined in 2001, and the support team. They avoided offering packaged solutions to clients, preferring instead to work through issues in an open-minded manner to reach a joint determination of what needed to be done. They also believed in operating with integrity, wanting clients to truly benefit from their work and being prepared to walk away if they did not believe they could make a difference.

In the early stages of VP's life this caused a degree of confusion, with some clients struggling to understand what was on offer. The consultants were generous with their time and expertise and not always rewarded for this. Despite these frustrations and the obvious temptation to 'productise' what VP offered, Court staunchly resisted packaging or closely labelling its practice. Gradually, as clients began to see the benefits of the VP approach, they shared their positive experience with others – and took it with them when they changed firms. Today, VP has a 'family tree' that charts the emergence of a wider VP circle of clients that have become, in effect, an extension of the VP 'family'.

As more clients came, more consultants were needed. Instead of recruiting, VP formed partnerships with a small number of experienced associates who worked with it flexibly according to demand and their other workloads. VP adopted an open and generous approach towards involving these associates in shaping

Figure 7 ■ Model of the values of Value Partnership

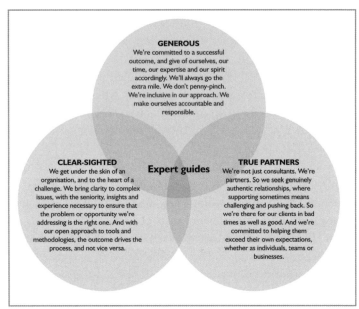

GENEROUS
We're committed to a successful outcome, and give of ourselves, our time, our expertise and our spirit accordingly. We'll always go the extra mile. We don't penny-pinch. We're inclusive in our approach. We make ourselves accountable and responsible.

CLEAR-SIGHTED
We get under the skin of an organisation, and to the heart of a challenge. We bring clarity to complex issues, with the seniority, insights and experience necessary to ensure that the problem or opportunity we're addressing is the right one. And with our open approach to tools and methodologies, the outcome drives the process, and not vice versa.

Expert guides

TRUE PARTNERS
We're not just consultants. We're partners. So we seek genuinely authentic relationships, where supporting sometimes means challenging and pushing back. So we're there for our clients in bad times as well as good. And we're committed to helping them exceed their own expectations, whether as individuals, teams or businesses.

work and sharing expertise. It also paid a better rate than the industry norm to boost its attractiveness to good people and to avoid putting its client reputation at risk.

After five years of steady year-on-year growth, during which the business doubled in size, the practice reached the limits of the associate model. Court and Rogers were exceptionally busy and it was becoming clear that an extended team of capable consultants was not enough for continued growth. The practice needed to take on more full-time partners who were capable and motivated to develop the business. These new partners had to be carefully recruited to sustain VP's values and way of working. There were few formulae that could be easily taught to newcomers. The fact that there is little pre-formulated content to the consulting model also makes it difficult for erstwhile competitors to copy VP's practice. In this regard, it is similar to YSC.

Growing the core team worked. VP trebled in size and is still growing strongly, enjoying an increase in revenues in 2011. It remains committed to its founding principles, with a vision for 2015 to reach a size that it believes maximises resilience in uncertain times. Beyond that, growth is not the main priority; the priorities are relevance, impact, reputation and sustainability.

VP's steady growth and secure base can clearly be attributed to the happy coincidence of values between clients and the VP team. In the words of its partners:

Value Partnership exists to help its clients to solve organisation critical challenges – ie, challenges that are organisational in nature, and critical in terms of their potential impact on the organisation itself. Our service is particularly suited to complex international businesses.

We possess a unique combination of qualities. We are clear-sighted, able to get quickly to the real heart of our clients' challenges. We are generous with our time and our effort. And we are true partners, building strong and lasting client relationships.

As a result, we work differently to most of our competitors; we are neither arms-length advisers nor embedded implementers. Instead we're expert guides, helping clients identify and implement the best route forward, standing beside them every step of the journey, and doing whatever it takes to enable them to attain their goal more successfully than they thought possible.

VP has always focused clearly on developing authentic, value-adding client relationships in the confident knowledge that the revenues will follow. The VP team has always preferred secure and steady growth to spectacular financial results or 'getting rich quick'.

Notes

1 Sense and nonsense

1 Peter M. Senge, *The Fifth Discipline: The Art and Practice of the Learning Organisation*, Random House, 2006.

2 Extracted from a talk by Sir Adrian Cadbury sponsored by The Foundation of Lady Katherine Leveson, 'Beliefs and Business: the experience of Quaker Companies', in the 'Faith Seeking Understanding' series, May 2003.

3 John Kay, *Obliquity*, Profile Books, 2010.

4 Mimi Schwartz and Sherron Watkins, *Power Failure: The Inside Story of The Collapse of Enron*, Crown Business, 2003.

5 Some of the findings were published in Julie Froud, Sukhdev Johal, Adam Leaver and Karel Williams, *Financialization and Strategy, Narrative and Numbers*, Routledge, 2006; others were presented by the author at seminars.

6 A term coined by Joseph Schumpeter in *Capitalism, Socialism and Democracy* (1942) to denote a 'process of industrial mutation that incessantly revolutionises the economic structure from within, incessantly destroying the old one, incessantly creating a new one'. He goes so

far as to say that the 'process of creative destruction is the essential fact about capitalism'. Unfortunately, while a great concept, this became one of the most overused buzzwords of the dotcom boom (and bust), with nearly every technology CEO talking about how creative destruction would replace the old economy with the new.

7   Francis Wheen, *How Mumbo Jumbo Conquered the World*, Harper Perennial, 2004.

8   William Ian Miller, *Losing It*, Yale University Press, 2011.

2 Perspectives

1   Arie de Geus, *The Living Company: Growth Learning and Longevity in Business*, Nicholas Brealey Publishing, 1999.

2   Gordon Donaldson and Jay William Lorsch, *Decision Making at the Top*, Basic Books, 1983.

3   James Collins and Jerry Porras, *Built to Last: Successful Habits of Visionary Companies*, HarperCollins, 1994.

4   Robert Hagstrom, *The Essential Buffett: Timeless Principles for the New Economy*, John Wiley & Sons, 2001.

5   Claude Bébéar, *Ils vont tuer le capitalisme*, Plon, 2003.

6   Scott Adams, *The Dilbert Principle*, HarperBusiness, 1996.

3 Underpinnings

1   Research studies by, among others, Andy Green of the London Institute of Education, Richard Wilkinson of the University of Nottingham and Kate Pickett of the University of York. And research into the Nordic model by Eric Einhorn of the University of Massachusetts.

2   Christopher Beem, *The Necessity of Politics: Reclaiming American Public Life*, Chicago University Press, 1999.

3   Robert Putnam, *Bowling Alone: The Collapse and Revival of American Community*, Simon & Schuster, 2000.

4   Douglas L. Kruse, Richard B. Freeman and Joseph R. Blasi, 'Do Workers Gain by Sharing? Employee Outcomes under

Employee Ownership, Profit Sharing, and Broad-Based Stock Options', National Bureau of Economic Research, 2010.

5 *Leader to Leader*, No. 12, spring 1999.

6 Denzil Rankine, *Why Acquisitions Fail*, Financial Times Management Briefings, 2001.

7 KPMG studies of acquisitions, *Unlocking Shareholder Value: The keys to success in M&A*, 1999 and 2002.

8 National Bureau of Economic Research, 'Do Shareholders in Acquiring Firms Gain from Acquisitions?', Working Paper No. 9253, August 2003.

9 *The life and times of the CEO*, Cranfield University Research Paper, 1999.

10 Julie Froud *et al.*, op. cit.

11 *It's time to take your SOX off*, Booz Allen Hamilton survey, 2005.

12 *The Role of the Board in Creating a High Performing Organisation*, PARC, 2005.

13 *Leader to Leader*, op. cit.

14 Gareth Morgan, *Imaginization: New Mindsets for Seeing, Organizing, and Managing*, Sage Publications, 1993.

4 Economic performance

1 David N. Fuller, *Value Creation: Theory and Practice*, VALUE Incorporated, 2001.

2 Michael Goold, Andrew Campbell and Marcus Alexander, *Corporate–Level Strategy: Creating Value in the Multibusiness Company*, John Wiley & Sons, 1994.

5 The contributions of the social sciences

1 Julie Froud *et al.*, op. cit.

2 Victor Vroom, *Work and Motivation: Expectancy Theory*, Jossey-Bass, 1995.

3 Two examples are Meredith Belbin, *Management Teams: Why They Succeed or Fail*, Butterworth-Heinemann, 1981;

and Dave Francis and Don Young, *Improving Work Groups: A Practical Manual for Team Building*, Jossey-Bass, 1992.
4 Gillian Tett, *Fool's Gold: How Unrestrained Greed Corrupted a Dream, Shattered Global Markets and Unleashed a Catastrophe*, Little, Brown, 2009.
5 Henry Mintzberg, *Structure in Fives: Designing Effective Organisations*, Prentice-Hall, 1993.
6 Gareth Morgan, *Images of Organization*, Sage Publications, 1997.
7 Gareth Morgan, *Imaginization*, op. cit.

6 Business psychology

1 Eric Berne, *Games People Play: The Psychology of Human Relationships*, Penguin Books, 1964.
2 Will Schutz, FIRO-B, Fundamental Interpersonal Relations Test, 1958.
3 Dave Francis and Don Young, op. cit.
4 Myers-Briggs Type Indicator (MBTI) assessment is a psychometric questionnaire designed to measure psychological preferences.
D.A. Kolb, *Experiential Learning: Experience as the Source of Learning and Development*, Prentice Hall, 1984.

7 Politics and power

1 Gerry Egan, *Working the Shadow Side*, Jossey-Bass, 1994.
2 Gareth Morgan, *Images of Organization*, op. cit.
Kurt Lewin, *Resolving Social Conflicts*, Harper and Row, 1948.

8 Synthesis

1 This material was originally compiled for a seminar by Ian Pringle, Don Young and Charlotte Young.
2 Ibid.

Acknowledgements

I am deeply in debt to many people, who gave me their valuable time and experience.

Special among them are:

- Ian Pringle, who is one of the smallish band of HR directors who understood business better than most CEOs and married this to a deep understanding of how to manage change through complex organisations. He was until recently joint CEO of TDG, an international logistics group.

- Paul Hewitt, who started life as an accountant helping small companies to IPOs and then moved to Euromoney, a publishing group, where he was one of a trio that took the business to a leading position in its markets. He became finance director of Redland, exposing the drastic destruction of value created by unwise acquisitions, before moving to the Co-operative Group as finance director and deputy CEO. He is now chair of a venture capital fund and a 'business angel' in his own right.

- Ken Rowe, Gurnek Bains and Charles Mead, directors of YSC, a leading business psychology consultancy. Charles first assessed me in the 1970s, which event led almost directly to the foundation of YSC in 1990. These three psychologists – two from a clinical psychology background, with later experience in social psychology, and one occupational psychologist with an early background in experimental psychology – helped in the writing of Chapter 6.

■ Malcolm Hatfield, long-time occupational psychologist and founder of the Association of Business Psychologists, who demonstrated that applied psychology is a better way of predicting future business success than financial spreadsheets.

■ Mike Regan and Simon Court, directors of Value Partnership. Mike was HR director of Electrolux AB. Simon founded Value Partnership with the close help of his wife Jane and a little from me.

■ Marcus Alexander, one of the few business academics who can hold his own in all respects (including carousing) with the toughest of managers and have them eating out of his hand.

■ Wendy Hirsh, who taught me that applied social sciences are a better way of understanding the antics of the banking industry than any other medium of analysis. She was an invaluable source of information on the behaviour of individuals, groups and tribes at work.

■ Charlotte Young, who forthrightly gave of her wisdom derived from being dean of the School of Management at the University of Westminster, director of management development at Thorn EMI, co-founder of YSC and, currently, chair of the School for Social Entrepreneurs. In this role, she received a Queen's Award for Enterprise Promotion in 2009.

- Lois Kelly, who has patiently and forthrightly provided editing support as well as valuable experience as an educator of middle managers.

- Mike Haffenden, director and founder of the Performance and Reward Centre and Corporate Research Forum, who sponsored much of the research and interviews behind the book. He brought his experience as HR director at Hewlett Packard.

- Last, but by no means least, David Lincoln, erstwhile director of the Towers Perrin HR practice and a former director of PARC.

Index